A NATURAL HISTORY ATLAS TO THE CAYS OF THE U.S. VIRGIN ISLANDS

A NATURAL HISTORY ATLAS TO THE CAYS OF THE U.S. VIRGIN ISLANDS

ARTHUR E. DAMMANN AND DAVID W. NELLIS

PINEAPPLE PRESS, INC.
SARASOTA, FLORIDA

This book is dedicated to George Seaman,
who preceded us as a Pittman-Robertson biologist and was one
of the few early supporters of Virgin Islands wildlife conservation.

A NATURAL HISTORY ATLAS TO THE CAYS OF THE
U.S. VIRGIN ISLANDS

All materials contained in this Atlas including, but not limited to text, photographs, drawings and illustrations, were supplied by and are the property of the Government of the Virgin Islands and/or the authors.

TEXT COPYRIGHT ©1992 BY GOVERNMENT OF THE
VIRGIN ISLANDS
PHOTOGRAPHS COPYRIGHT © 1992 (EXCEPT THOSE
OTHERWISE ATTRIBUTED) BY DAVID W. NELLIS
ALL RIGHTS RESERVED

ALL RIGHTS RESERVED. NO PART OF THIS BOOK MAY BE REPRODUCED IN ANY FORM OR BY ANY MEANS, ELECTRONIC OR MECHANICAL, INCLUDING PHOTOCOPYING, RECORDING, OR BY ANY INFORMATION STORAGE AND RETRIEVAL SYSTEM, WITHOUT PERMISSION IN WRITING FROM THE PUBLISHER, EXCEPT BY A REVIEWER WHO MAY QUOTE BRIEF PASSAGES IN A REVIEW.

PUBLISHED BY
PINEAPPLE PRESS, INC.
DRAWER 16008
SOUTHSIDE STATION
SARASOTA, FLORIDA 34239

Library of Congress Cataloging-in-Publication Data
Dammann, Arthur E.
A natural history atlas to the cays of the U.S. Virgin Islands / Arthur E. Dammann and David W. Nellis ; Virgin Islands Department of Planning and Natural Resources, Division of Fish and Wildlife.
p. cm.
Includes bibliographical references and index.
ISBN 1-56164-022-0 : $24.95
1. Natural history -- Virgin Islands of the United States -- Maps. 2. Ecology -- Virgin Islands of the United States. -- Maps. I. Nellis, David W. II. Virgin Islands of the United States. Division of Fish and Wildlife. III. Pineapple Press, Inc. IV. Title.
G1046.D1D3 1992 <G&M>
508.7297'22--dc20
92-23127
CIP
MAP

First Edition   10   9   8   7   6   5   4   3   2   1

DESIGN BY
ROBERT FLEURY

Typography by Millicent Hampton-Shepherd
Printed in Hong Kong

Acknowledgments

This atlas has been prepared with funds from the U.S. Department of the Interior, Fish and Wildlife Service, Pittman-Robertson Federal Aid Project FW-5, Job Title, "Study of the Wildlife Potential of the Virgin Island Cays."

Materials from other studies of the Virgin Islands have been acknowledged by citation in the text and used freely throughout the atlas. We wish to thank the following for use of the results of their efforts:

Virgin Islands Departments of Agriculture and of Conservation and Cultural Affairs; Virgin Islands Planning Office, and the Virgin Islands Soil and Water Conservation District; University of the Virgin Islands, Caribbean Research Institute; The United States Department of Agriculture's Soil Conservation Service; United States Army Corps of Engineers; United States Department of the Interior's National Park Service; Virgin Islands National Park; the students and faculty of Hackley and Masters schools; and the many residents of the Virgin Islands who displayed an interest in the project. Of special significance are the contributions made by Dr. Richard Philibosian and John Yntema.

Common names generally follow the Checklist of Vertebrates of the United States, the U.S. Territories and Canada, which in itself is a compilation of generally accepted checklists for the various taxonomic groups. Scientific names for species mentioned can be found in the Glossary of Scientific and Common Names. Local common names have been added when appropriate.

All the photographs are by David Nellis except as noted. The photographs have been accumulated over a period of years under many different lighting conditions.

Table of

9
Preface

10
Locations of breeding sea birds

11
Introduction

19
The cays

139
Glossary of place names

155
References

157
Index to species

159
General index

CONTENTS

THE CAYS

20-21
BOOBY ROCK

22-23
BOVONI CAY

24-25
BUCK ISLAND
Near St. Croix

26-27
BUCK ISLAND
Near St. Thomas

28-29
CAPELLA ISLAND

30-31
CARVEL ROCK

32-33
CAS CAY

34-35
CINNAMON CAY

36-37
COCKROACH CAY

38-39
COCOLOBA CAY

40-41
CONGO CAY

42-43
CRICKET ROCK

44-45
CURRENT ROCK

46-47
DOG ISLAND

48-49
DUTCHCAP CAY

50-51
FISH CAY

52-53
FLANAGAN ISLAND

54-55
FLAT CAY

56-57
FRENCHCAP CAY

58-59
GRASS CAY

60-61
GREAT ST. JAMES ISLAND

62-63
GREEN CAY
St. Croix

64-65
GREEN CAY
St. Thomas

66-67
HANS LOLLICK ISLAND

68-69
HASSEL ISLAND

70-71
HENLEY CAY

72-73
INNER BRASS ISLAND

74-75
KALKUN CAY

76-77
LEDUCK ISLAND

78-79
LITTLE HANS LOLLICK ISLAND

80-81
LITTLE ST. JAMES ISLAND

82-83
LOVANGO CAY

84-85
MINGO CAY

86-87
OUTER BRASS ISLAND

88-89
PATRICIA CAY

90-91
PELICAN CAY

92-93
PERKINS CAY

94-95
PROTESTANT CAY

96-97
RAMGOAT CAY

98-99
RATA CAY

100-101
ROTTO CAY

102-103
SABA ISLAND

104-105
SAIL ROCK

106-107
SALT CAY

108-109
SAVANA ISLAND

110-111
SHARK ISLAND

112-113
STEVEN CAY

114-115
SULA CAY

116-117
THATCH CAY

118-119
TRUNK CAY

120-121
TURTLEDOVE CAY

122-123
TWO BROTHERS

124-125
WATER ISLAND

126-127
WATERLEMON CAY

128-129
WEST CAY

130-131
WHISTLING CAY

132-133
MANGLARS

134-135
MAN-MADE/DESTROYED ISLANDS

136-137
UNVEGETATED ROCKS

THE U.S. VIRGIN ISLANDS

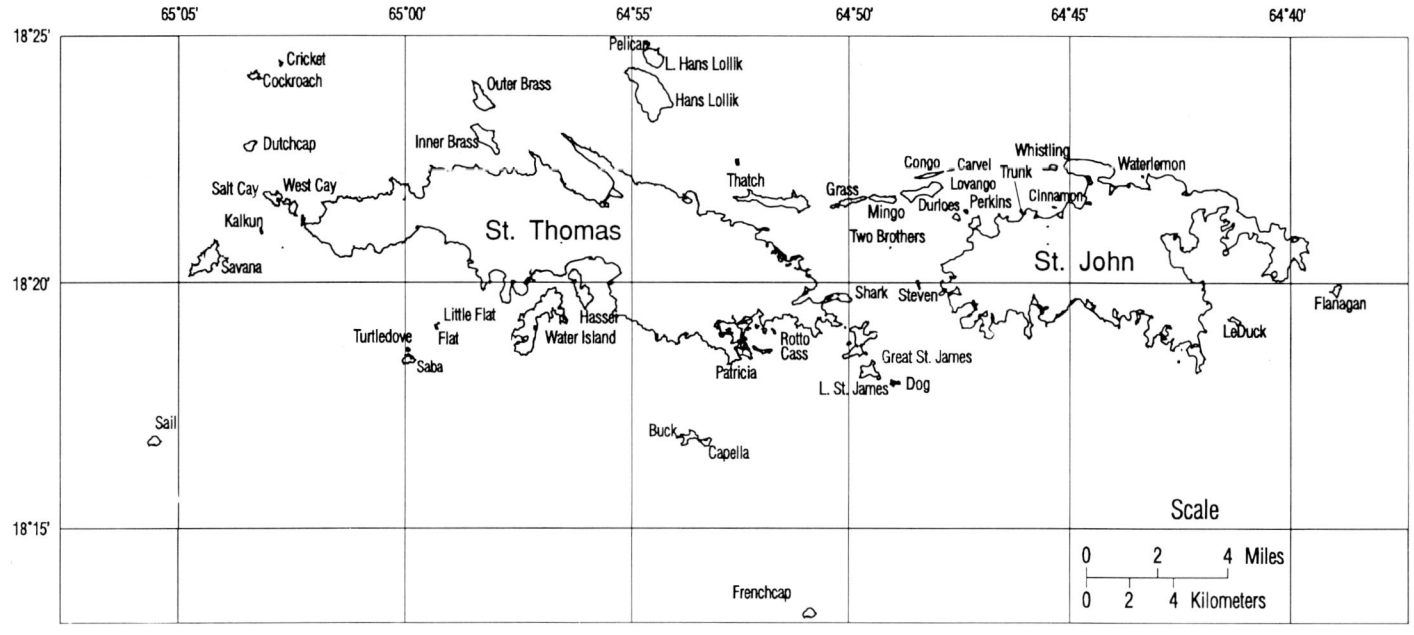

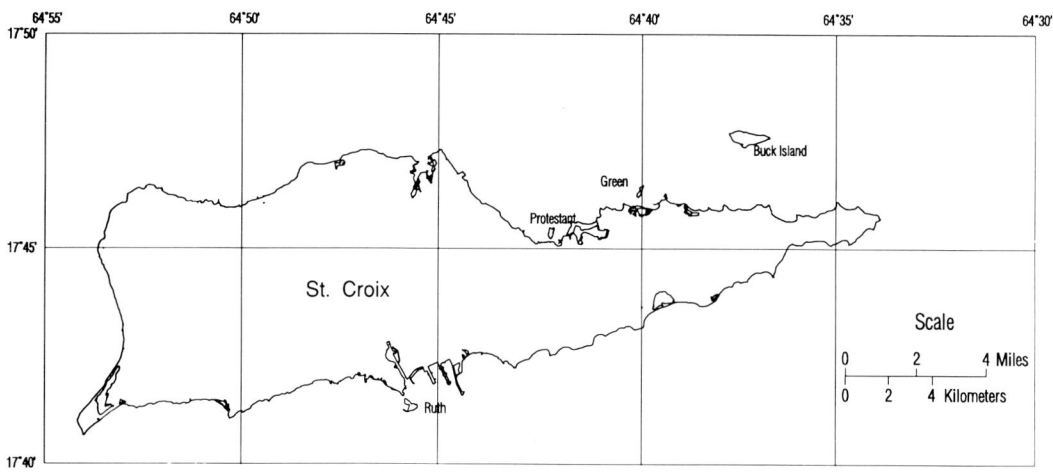

PREFACE

Rupert Rock

As human populations expand worldwide, competition mounts among most other biological populations for space and the other necessities of life. Both terrestrial and aquatic plants and animals are subjected to incidental as well as deliberate harassment and disturbance. Air pollution, water pollution, noise pollution, earth changes, introduced species, and other man-related factors limit their numbers and geographical ranges, sometimes to the point of extinction.

In the U.S. Virgin Islands, such changes are rapid, drastic, and usually irreversible. There is no place to run, no place to hide. It seems impossible and perhaps undesirable to stop this process of development on the three main islands. However, the small land masses offshore offer possibilities for a different set of uses. The information compiled in this atlas is intended to encourage rational decisions for resource management.

Recommendations are made in accordance with Act 4104 of the Twelfth Legislature of the Virgin Islands of the United States in Regular Session 1978. The title of the Act is "To Transfer the Management, Control and Use of Certain Government-Owned Offshore Islands and Cays to the Department of Conservation and Cultural Affairs and to Preserve Such Islands and Cays as Wildlife Sanctuaries and for Recreational Use." The Statement of Motives reads: "As the population of the islands of St. Thomas, St. John and St. Croix continues to increase rapidly and urbanization of these islands expands, the Legislature recognizes the great natural resources provided by the offshore islands and cays that dot Virgin Island waters. While many of these islands and cays, the majority of which are owned by the Virgin Islands Government, are little used or cared for at present, they enhance the scenic beauty and vistas of the Virgin Islands, provide habitats for rapidly disappearing species of birds and other animals, and many have fine beaches or beach sites potentially useful as public recreational facilities. Since the Department of Conservation and Cultural Affairs* is charged with the governmental responsibility of protecting natural resources, wildlife preservation and restoration, and the development of recreational facilities, it is appropriate that the jurisdiction, management, and control of such offshore islands and cays be transferred to such Department for the public good and general welfare of present and future generations of Virgin Islanders."

The Department has since been reorganized as the Department of Planning and Natural Resources.

LOCATIONS OF BREEDING SEA BIRDS

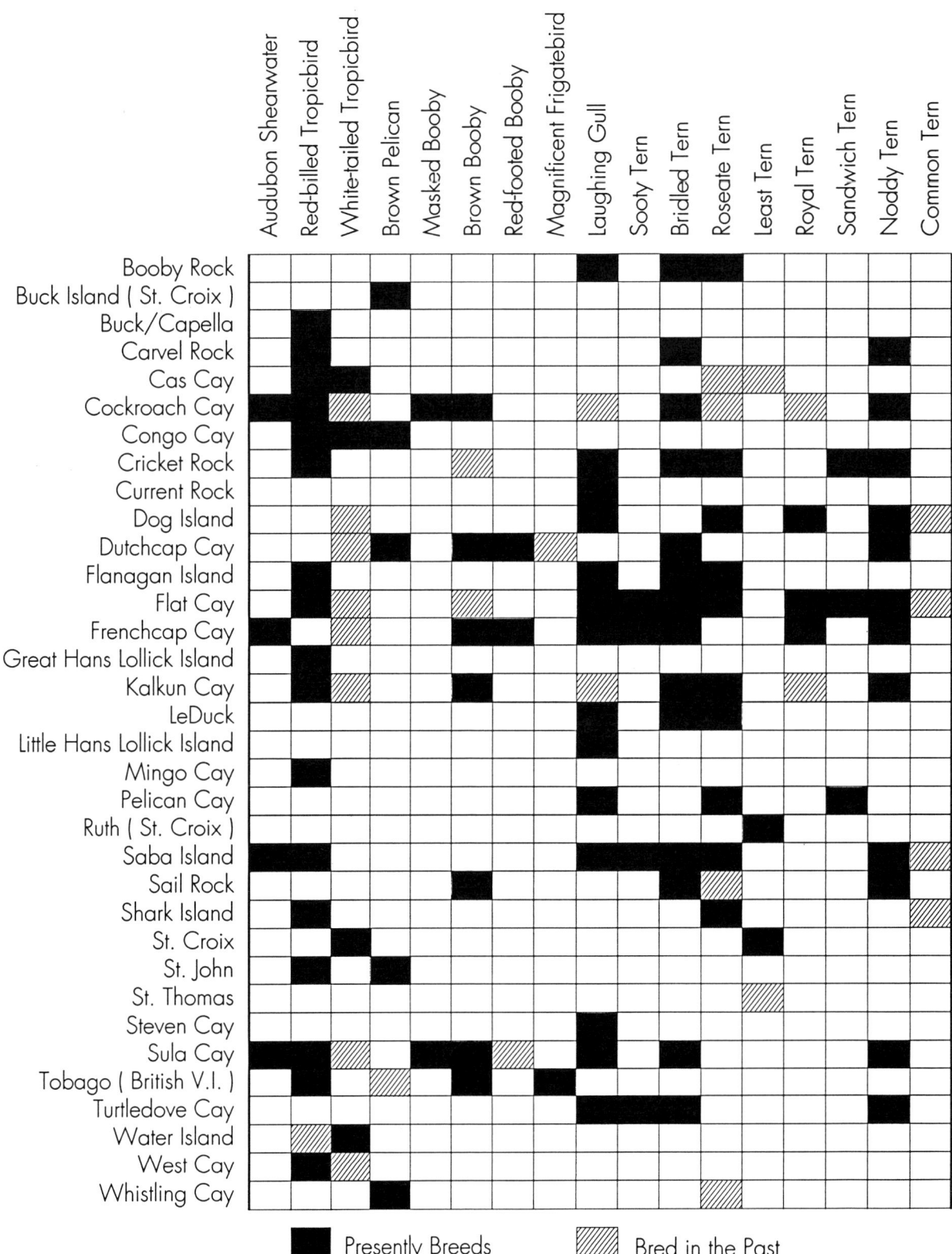

Introduction

Shorelines

The percentage of the total shoreline of these small masses is far more important than their area. The "actual" or tidal shoreline including all "bay/estuary" measurements is more biologically meaningful than the often quoted "general coastline" figure which largely ignores the indentations and is measured from point to point. The following figures given by the U.S. Army Corps of Engineers are for the "total" shoreline.

St. Croix has 70.3 miles (113 km) of shoreline, St. Thomas has 52.8 (85 km), and St. John 49.7 miles (80 km). The total shoreline for these three islands is 172.8 miles (278 km). The total for all the other smaller units in the U.S. Virgin Islands is 61 miles (98 km). The small land masses then can be described as a "fourth shoreline" approximately equal in magnitude to that of any one of the main islands.

The total shoreline length of the U.S. Virgin Islands is thus 233.8 miles (376 km). This length may be compared to Florida's 2,989 miles (4,809 km). Of the total shoreline, sandy beaches make up 21% (11.1 miles, 17.8 km) of St. Thomas, 43% (30.3 miles, 48.7 km) of St. Croix, 10% (3.0 miles, 4.8 km) of St. John, and 8% (4.8 miles, 7.7 km) of the smaller land masses. In all there are about 50 miles (80 km) of sandy beaches in the islands. These beaches are not only important as places of recreation and aesthetic beauty for people, but they also form a distinct habitat for many species of plants and animals. Moreover, they are a part of the few remaining nesting sites for endangered marine turtles in the entire Atlantic Ocean and Caribbean Sea.

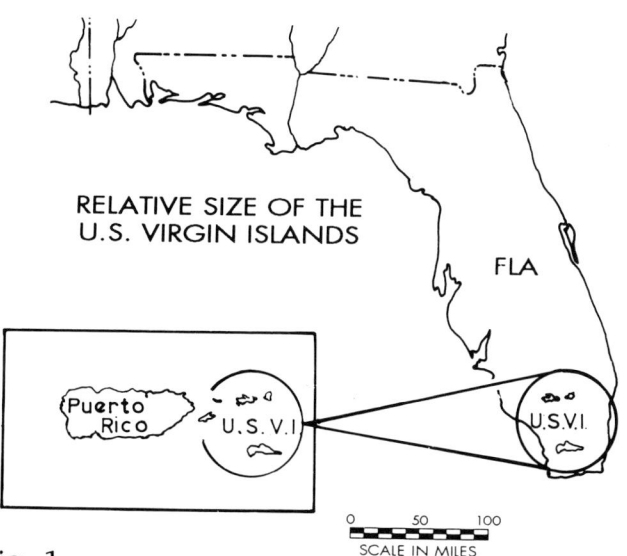

Fig. 1

It is worth remembering that the entire U.S. Virgin Islands, including the submerged shelf, would fit into Everglades National Park (2,020 sq. mi.) (Fig. 1) or the entire geological platform into Chesapeake Bay, which is about 190 miles long by 20 miles wide and has more than 5,000 miles of shoreline.

Climate and Plants

The climate of the Virgin Islands can be classified as "dry-tropical"; whereas the vegetation of all the smaller islands comes under the general heading of "subtropical dry forest." The controlling factors are high insolation; warm temperatures; low, irregular rainfall; and virtually constant easterly, daytime tradewinds. These combine to create a high evapo-transpiration rate and soil-moisture deficits. Much of the rain falls in brief showers, so that it rapidly evaporates from the surface of the soil and vegetation. This is particularly true on the windward-facing slopes and is discussed in more detail below. Bowden et al. (1970) give the annual average rainfall for the main islands as 41 inches (104 cm) per year and that of the outer cays and islands as "between 30 and 35 inches" (75 to 85 cm). However, as just mentioned, rainfall per se constitutes a poor criterion on which to judge vegetational structure, and 30 or 40 inches (75 to 100 cm) of rain in a relatively cool, windless area produces far more lush vegetation than the same rainfall produces in a hot, windy one.

In the Virgin Islands, as elsewhere in the northern hemisphere except at high latitudes and very high elevations, north-facing slopes are cooler and more heavily vegetated because they receive less insolation, and thus evapo-transpiration is less than on sunnier south-facing slopes. Ravines, other depressions and channels of intermittent streams, and the leeward side of hills are all protected from the drying effect of the wind; in these places vegetation is heavier.

On steep slopes with little or no soil, run-off is rapid. If these slopes are south-facing and exposed to the wind, only a few species of the most drought-resistant plants can exist. Vegetation near the waterline is further influenced by salt spray and splash on a daily, seasonal, and storm-induced basis.

Vegetational cover indicates the amount of moisture actually

Introduction

available for use by the plants, rather than the total rainfall. Figure 2 is a semi-diagrammatic illustration of these relationships. As one travels by boat through the islands, many peaks and headlands exhibit the depicted features almost as diagrammatically as the drawing. Cooling effects of elevation are noticeable only at the highest altitudes of the three major islands.

Using Holdridge's (1947) method, Ewel and Whitmore (1973) place all the small land masses discussed here, except one, into the classification of "sub-tropical dry forest."

The variables used by Holdridge to delineate any given life zone are a) mean annual precipitation and b) the mean annual temperature range within which most plants carry on maximum photosynthesis (32° to 86° F; 8° to 30° C). The relationship of these two factors controls the available moisture and resulting plant growth as previously discussed. Savana Island is the only area, other than parts of each of the three major islands, which is classified as "sub-tropical moist forest" by this system; we suspect on the basis of our own observations that this classification of Savana is largely an artifact.

A more interesting and meaningful classification of vegetative types for small areas was adopted by Robertson (1957) in describing the vegetation of St. John. Throughout the rest of our descriptive material Robertson's categories will be used.

In his discussion, Robertson adopted the following descriptive names: moist forest, dry forest, dry forest with cactus, cactus woodland, croton-acacia scrub, wind-flattened scrub, mangrove, and beach vegetation. He included a list of "characteristic" species for each category. In our own subsequent work, however, we found a great deal of overlapping, with most species widely distributed from sea level to mountaintops. The taxonomic groups making up most of his categories differ chiefly in their relative abundance at a given location. There are, however, a few fairly reliable indicator species which will be used in the following discussions.

Historic Changes

It seems that in pre-Columbian times the main islands, at least, were covered with closed-canopy forests and possessed permanent, if small, freshwater streams. There are remnant populations of secondary freshwater fish, including eels, and edible freshwater crustaceans of the genus *Macrobrachium* on all three main islands. During the pre-Columbian period, the forests probably possessed the

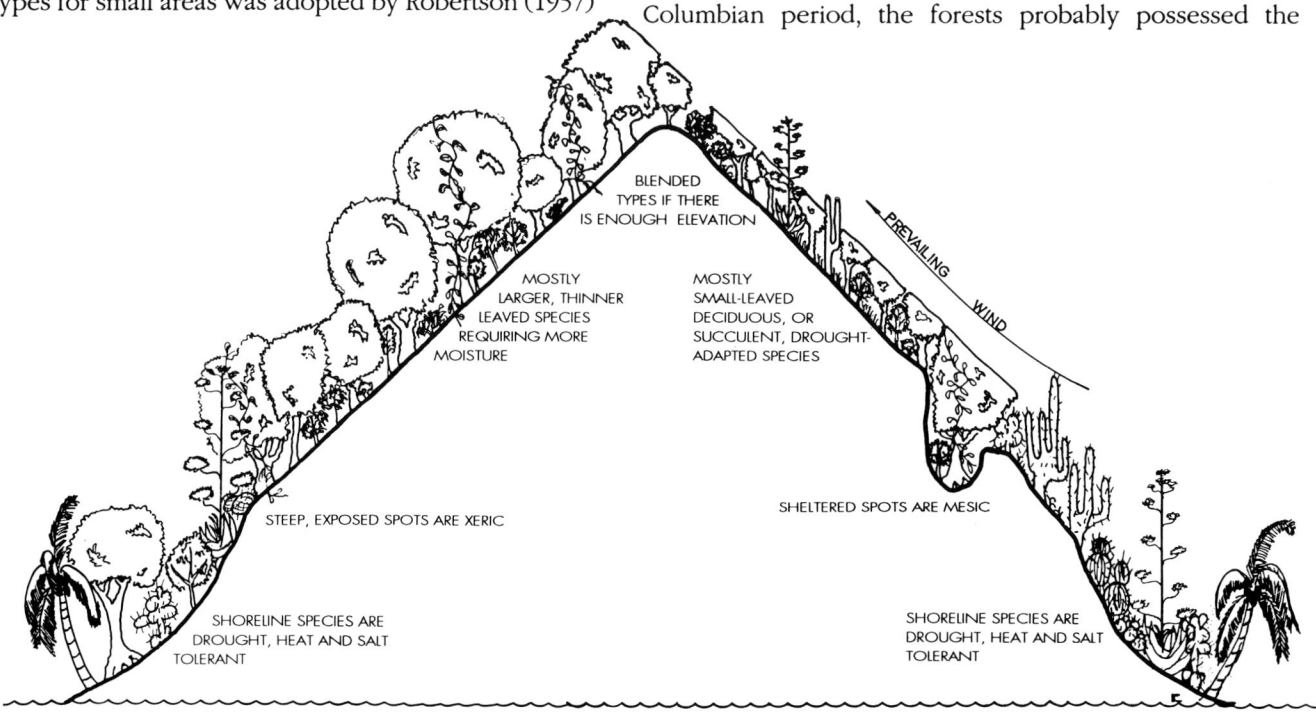

SEMIDIAGRAMMATIC PROFILE OF HILL, SHOWING EFFECT OF WIND ON VEGETATIVE STRUCTURE AND SPECIES COMPOSITION

Fig. 2

Introduction

characteristics and species composition of sub-tropical moist forests. Under those conditions the xerophytes were probably confined to south-facing and steep windward slopes of nearly bare rock or shallow pockets of soil, and to xeric shoreline strands.

The aboriginal Indians probably made little impact on these forests. However, when Europeans began the colonization process with subsequent cutting, burning, plowing, grazing, and road construction, a long chain of related events was initiated that continues at an accelerating pace today.

When the canopy is opened, insolation increases and the shallow soil heats up rapidly, thus increasing the evaporation rate, drying out the soil, and eventually lowering the water table. As a result, only the drought-adapted plants from the shorelines and steep south-facing slopes are able to recolonize the opening. After the meager nutrients have been used up by agricultural crops, the site is often abandoned. Grazing by sheep and goats aggravates the situation: because rain water cannot penetrate soil that has been compacted by the hooves of these animals, run-off and erosion of the already shallow soil results. Because animals are often allowed to overgraze, it is a common practice to burn the encroaching xerophytic underbrush in order to encourage grasses. The result of this sequence is that species that require moist soil either disappear or become restricted to the remaining spots that provide enough moisture. At the same time, those species which possess wide-spreading, shallow root systems that can take advantage of brief showers and are able to endure the insolation, high surface temperatures, and soil-moisture deficit, enlarge their ranges.

Plant ecologists with whom we have talked are convinced that this sequence of events is what has happened over large areas of the Middle East and Africa. They further maintain that when a forested area is denuded, the rainfall pattern is disrupted, and, as a result, the area becomes increasingly arid. They attribute this to the total effect of increased soil temperatures, differences in the radiated heat load to the atmosphere above the area, and differences in the contribution of evapo-transpiration to the moisture load of the atmosphere in the immediate vicinity.

Since the Virgin Islands are essentially mountain peaks protruding from the sea, and since they display the "island effect" whereby cloud masses build up over each small land mass more often than over the surrounding sea, it seems possible that this island effect is altered by the changes in surface characteristics of the islands themselves as described for the countries in the Middle East. This may partially account for the seemingly gradual "drying out" of many of the islands of the eastern Caribbean in historic times.

A further characteristic of sub-tropical and tropical forests contributes to the extinction of species under these last conditions. A forest at these latitudes is generally made up of hundreds of species of trees, rather than the few species characteristic of forests at higher latitudes. Two individuals of the same species are sometimes several miles apart. As these individuals are destroyed by removal, or die because of habitat changes, the population becomes so small, and suitable habitat so limited, that reproduction is not possible and the species disappears. The probability of this happening on small islands is very high because such islands may have only a few individuals of each species under original conditions.

It is not easy to extend this generalized picture from the main islands to the smaller cays for several reasons. The cays are too small to have ever sustained permanent freshwater streams, given the rainfall in the area during the time for which there are consistent weather records (less than 100 years). Their underground water capacity is also much less. Furthermore, a larger percentage of their area is subject to the desiccating effect of the wind and salt water. None of them attains the altitudes of the main islands. The highest point of St. Croix is 1,165 feet (355 m), on St. Thomas 1,550 feet (472 m), and on St. John 1,277 feet (389 m). Among the cays, the highest elevation occurs on Great Hans Lollik (704 feet, 215 m). Hans Lollick also supports the most mature forest of any of the cays.

The cays are also too small to have ever sustained populations of all the species of plants and animals known on the larger islands. We thus have less confidence in our ideas about their pre-Columbian characteristics, because all but the very smallest of them have been used for grazing goats and sheep since the earliest times of colonization, and

Introduction

grazing has often been accompanied by periodic burning at various times extending to the present. Several cays have been inhabited by people who have further modified them. For these reasons, they cannot really be used as "natural laboratories" to interpret the sequence of events on the larger islands. Most of them, however, are refugia for a number of species of plants and animals under today's conditions. The term "refugia" connotes the idea that plant and animal species have "gone" there to hide. The true situation can only be understood in terms of the biogeography of the islands and the effects of past geological events and climates.

All the northern Virgin Islands, including the British ones, are located on the same geological "bank" or "shelf" with Puerto Rico. They are geologically the easternmost extension of the Greater Antillean Chain, of which Cuba, Jamaica, and Hispaniola are the larger emergent land masses. Each of these large islands, however, is separated from the others by deep trenches.

The largest and highest of the Greater Antilles have been above water since at least the end of the Tertiary period, some one million years ago, and much of the emergent land mass may be 60 million years old. However, of more immediate interest to our discussion is that, beginning about then and continuing until barely 10,000 years ago, a situation has resulted in which, at various times, each of the islands (except the St. Croix shelf), cays, and rocks of the Virgin Islands has been connected with one another and with Puerto Rico, Vieques, and Culebra. When Puerto Rico and the Virgin Islands together composed a virtually continuous land mass, that mass had a common biota, or association of plants and animals. Each of the species, however, occupied its own ecologic niche and geographic range.

St. Croix is situated on its own bank and is surrounded by very deep water. At one time the emergent land mass was large enough to include all areas within the 100-fathom curve. This means that Buck Island, Protestant Cay, Green Cay, the shoal areas to the south, and all of Lang Bank to the east were part of St. Croix and had a common biota which was, and is, different from that of the northern Virgins.

A further complication of the picture is that all the islands of both the Greater and Lesser Antillean chains are probably "oceanic" islands. That is, they have probably never been connected to a continental land mass. The implications of this are that they arose from the sea as bare rock, that they have developed all their soil structure since then, and that they have acquired their original biotas by chance invasion and establishment of "continental" species of plants and animals. The routes of invasion have led both from the Yucatan Peninsula of Mexico to the Greater Antilles and from Venezuela and Trinidad to the Lesser Antilles. Evolution has been at work all this time, and, together with the past geological events, it determines the species of plants and animals to be found on each of the islands and cays today, provided of course that we allow for the actions of man.

The pre-Columbian Indians carried both plants and animals as food and, in all probability, introduced such species as the red-footed tortoise, the agouti (a large rodent), and cassava to the American Virgin Islands. Other species came on the slave ships and trading vessels. In relatively recent times a great many ornamental trees, shrubs, and vines have been intentionally introduced so that the urban vegetation looks much the same as that of any other urban area in the tropics around the world.

The classic book *The Theory of Island Biogeography* (MacArthur and Wilson 1967) delves deeply into the facts, philosophies, and theories of the distribution of plants and animals on islands. Organisms that can fly or be carried by the wind (birds, bats, some insects, spiders, and some plant seeds, etc.) or by some flying animal (plant seeds carried by birds) have the best chance to colonize the islands. Those which must be rafted across long expanses of salt water have a more difficult time. The least likely of all to colonize an oceanic island (an island that has never been connected to a continent) are the very large terrestrial animals which would require a "raft" of a huge size. For this reason the large land mammals (big cats, tapirs, horses, elephants, etc.) are not to be expected as colonizers of such islands, nor are primary freshwater fishes that cannot tolerate salt water. Where large terrestrial animals exist or have existed, on oceanic islands the fossil record shows that they have evolved locally from smaller ancestors.

Probability of colonization of an island is also a function of its size and distance from the source of colonizing organisms. Small islands far from the source have lower probabilities than larger islands closer to the source. Moreover, each invading species has a critical minimum area requirement

Introduction

below which it cannot maintain a population. Thus the biota of an island is directly related to the size of the island.

The relationship between the ecological conditions present on the islands and the ecological needs of the colonizer are strong controlling factors. If either the climate, soil, water, or some other factor is not "right" for the colonizer, or if its ecological niche is already filled by another organism, its chance of establishment is virtually zero.

Today, thousands of years after their emergence from the sea, the islands exhibit the effects of wind, weather, the action of the sea, and the actions of man. On the side exposed to the open sea are tall cliffs produced by wave action. The vegetation line is high above normal water levels since winter storms to the north send huge waves surging high up the cliff faces. On the cays to the north of the main islands these rock faces are mostly located on the northern and eastern shores. These cliffs provide some of the most important nesting areas for sea birds. The sides of the cays that are best protected from the large winter seas are often sloping, with the vegetation line much closer to the water level. Here are the nesting sites of terrestrial birds such as doves, wild pigeons, and others.

Salt Ponds

The sides of the cays that do possess a gently sloping run-off surface frequently have "salt ponds" at the foot of valleys. These ponds are somewhat variable in their origin and structure, but most of them are separated from the sea by a berm or dike, which is usually composed of storm-tossed coral rubble and sand. Today, as at any period of time, it is possible to observe all stages in the life cycle of salt ponds. It is presently popular in certain quarters to attribute the health of existing coral reefs to the presence of salt ponds. In actuality, a pond is born as the result of the growth of corals across the mouth of an indentation in the shoreline. Thus the pond, which originally contributed nothing to the reef, may eventually, in fact, trap nutrients that would otherwise contribute to reef growth. Accretion and the influence of storms eventually form a berm separating the pond from the sea. A pond "dies" when it becomes so full of trapped debris that it is simply a playa behind the beach.

Until vegetational succession can re-forest such a playa its value as a "sediment trap" is highly variable. The life span of these transient ponds depends not only on such things as the amount of rainfall and vegetational cover of the slopes above them but also on the constantly changing relative sea level. In fairly short periods a pond can either be elevated or submerged again as part of the ocean in a continually fluctuating environment. In some cases (perhaps those which are younger) the dike is porous and the water level of the pond remains near sea level. However, the water level of many others is controlled by rainfall and evaporation. During severe droughts, some dry completely, while others become caked with salt, which is deposited in large crystals as the evaporation proceeds—hence the name "salt pond." These ponds are a prime habitat for shorebirds, ducks, and other waterbirds which feed, nest, and rest here. Their usual fringe of black, white, and buttonwood mangroves is the habitat of other birds such as herons, egrets, cuckoos, and pigeons. Hummingbirds frequently nest on branches overhanging the water. True ponds not connected to the sea have no red mangroves.

Unless the ponds have been secondarily opened to the sea by storm action or the work of man, they do not contain fish. Their biota is adapted to highly variable salinity, temperature, and oxygen concentration which marine fish find intolerable. During periods of low salinity a few species of aquatic insects such as mosquitos, water boatmen, and beetles utilize the ponds. At other times population explosions of brine shrimp turn them brick red. The silty bottoms harbor a variety of burrowing worms and other invertebrates tolerant of the low oxygen and high hydrogen sulphide concentrations. Algal plankton blooms are characteristic. It is this biota which contributes to the diet of shorebirds. If the ponds are opened to the sea the water quality changes enough for them to be invaded by fish. The new combination of predators and water quality changes the aquatic biota just described. The former ponds then afford valuable marine habitat of a kind that is otherwise scarce in the Virgin Islands.

It is possible (some say probable) that in a few years many or most ponds will again become part of the sea because of rising sea levels as glaciers melt from a manmade warming climate (greenhouse effect).

Introduction

Soils

The soils of the cays surrounding St. Thomas, St. John, and St. Croix have been reported on by the Soil Conservation Service of the U.S. Department of Agriculture (Rivera et al. 1970). In general, this study shows severe soil deficiencies for building and agriculture on the cays. Details for each cay are given in the account. Soil types also partly determine the vegetative types and species composition of the vegetation. Figure 3 lists the soil types and their abbreviations used in the text.

Soil Type	Description
CrE	Cramer gravelly clay loam, 12 to 40 percent slopes.
CrF	Cramer gravelly clay loam, 40 to 60 percent slopes.
CsE2	Cramer stoney clay loam, 12 to 40 percent slopes. Fifty to seventy percent of the surface is covered with stones.
CsF	Cramer stoney clay loam, 40 to 60 percent slopes.
DeD	Descalabrado clay loam, 20 to 40 percent slopes.
JuB	Jaucas sand, 0 to 5 percent slopes composed of sand-sized particles of coral, shells, and calcarious algae.
Ma	Made land.
SaC	San Anton clay loam, 5 to 12 percent slopes. Erosion can be severe when not protected by vegetation.
SgE	Southgate clay loam 12 to 40 percent slopes; a shallow slightly acid soil over granite.
SgF	Southgate clay loam, 40 to 60 percent slopes.
SrF	Southgate rock complex, 20 to 60 percent slopes. Soils are less than 5 inches thick and are between 50 to 70 percent rock outcrops.
Tf	Tidal flats, nearly level, barren areas that are periodically covered by tidal water.
Ts	Tidal swamp, clay or carbonate soil usually covered with salt water and a thick growth of mangrove trees.
Vr	Volcanic rock, 60 to 70 percent slopes. Between the outcrops is very shallow gravelly loam.

Fig. 3

Islands, Cays and Rocks

In the pictorial account of the "small land masses" which follows, the alphabetical arrangement was chosen for a number of reasons. First, we have been unable to discover criteria that will in all cases separate a "cay" from an "island" or a "rock." Size cannot be used; it can be seen that "Sail Rock" is larger than several "cays" and that "Dog Island" and "Le Duck Island" are smaller than either "Sail Rock" or most of the north shore "cays" near St. Thomas.

We considered the presence or absence of woody vegetation to be important biologically since, for one thing, it should be an indicator of stability and of absence of regular coverage by wave action or heavy spray. In general, most "rocks" should be small and free of vegetation. However, "Booby Rock" is vegetated, "Carvel Rock" has two small fig trees, and "Sail Rock" has only cactus and moss and certainly is not regularly covered by waves or spray.

Even alphabetical arrangement poses severe problems because each of the entities bears several names in each of several languages. These names are often duplicative. Thus, in English, there are several "Buck Islands" and "Bird Cays" in the American Virgins. If equivalent foreign language names are added, the duplication becomes formidable. Our glossary (see page 139) is an extraction of those names given by McGuire, 1925.

In the end we finally grouped as "rocks" all land masses that are small enough to be covered by wave action. Their only geological significance to terrestrial organisms seems to be that of providing temporary resting places for seabirds. Many of them are routinely used by gulls, terns, boobies, and pelicans. On occasion, herons and egrets also take advantage of them. A few submerged "rocks" are included in the glossary for the sake of completeness and to clarify the use of their names in the literature and on navigational charts.

Introduction

Mangroves

One other category of "islands" needs to be considered. These are the "mangrove islands" that do not contain any dry land. The term "manglar" has been used as a name for this type of formation. These small, dense masses of red mangrove trees are generally unnamed but are very important biologically because they are heavily used by birds of many kinds (the white-crowned pigeon is virtually dependent on them): some also have lizards of the genera Anolis and Iguana in them. It is doubtful that these egg-laying lizards can reproduce under the conditions found in manglars, but they do provide an interesting example of the invasion of new "islands" across short expanses of salt water.

The term "mangrove" requires some explanation to most nonbotanists. It is not the name for a particular tree but rather a generalized name given to a woody plant formation which is composed of several different families and many species of plants around the world. This assemblage of plants is tolerant of seawater; at least one species (red mangrove) grows on prop-roots which are permanently immersed in water, and it habitually grows in normal seawater. A succession of species from open seawater to the zone just above high tide is typical. These species gradually replace one another as soil and debris accumulate around their roots and render the resulting drier land uninhabitable for them. In the Virgin Islands, four species of shrubs and trees belonging to three different plant families are called "mangrove." These are commonly referred to as red mangrove, white mangrove, black mangrove and buttonwood mangrove. They are land builders and their formations tend to expand seaward.

Mangroves contribute significantly to the basic marine food chain in tropical areas. Their roles as a nursery area for fisheries, and in the protection of uplands from storm winds and surge, are also significant.

Human Influence

Entire "cays" have been eradicated and/or created by the actions of man. Krause Cay, which separated Krause Lagoon (Fig. 4) from the sea, was obliterated at the same time as the lagoon. The former Kraus Lagoon on the south shore of St. Croix was the crown jewel of mangrove forests in the Virgin Islands before being destroyed in the 1960s to make way for one of the world's largest oil refineries and a bauxite processing plant. It was a marvelously productive area for marine creatures and was the home of thousands of white-crowned pigeons. The birds were so numerous that hunters came from around the world on shooting forays. It was an extensive system of manglars and cays interspersed by numerous channels and bays opening to the sea yet offering perfect protection from the ravages of the open sea. Under present laws the area would have been absolutely protected.

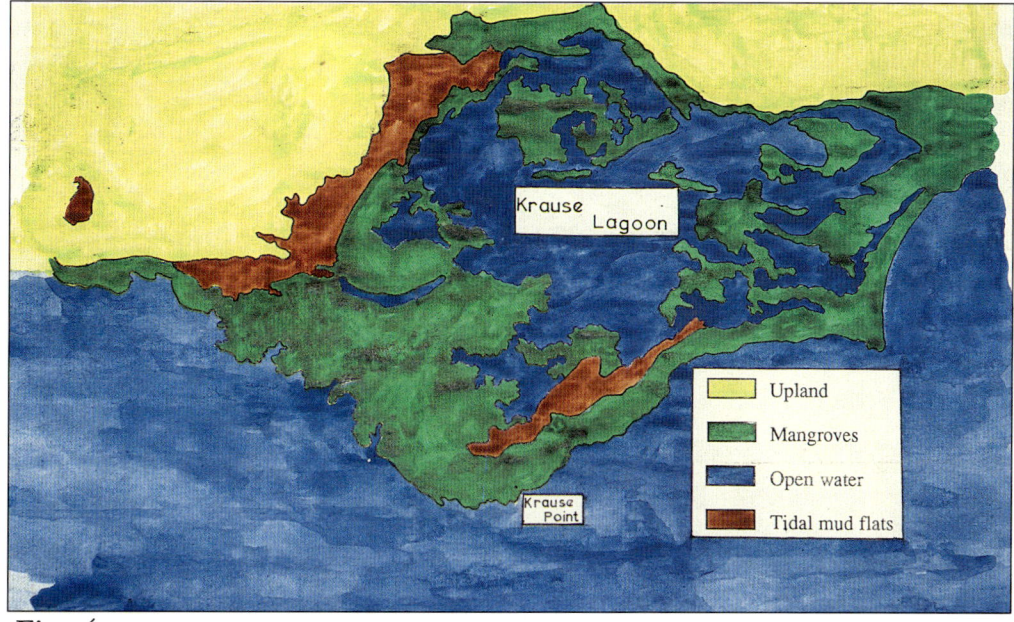

Fig. 4

Introduction

The dredge spoil from the shipping channel which has replaced Krause Lagoon was stockpiled offshore and now forms a "spoil island" which has been colonized by terrestrial vegetation and is used by pigeons, doves, and seabirds. This low-lying mass of unconsolidated material has survived the wave action and currents of a major hurricane and will probably persist for a long period of time. It is at least as biologically important as other naturally formed cays or islands.

The special cases mentioned above are grouped together at the end of the alphabetically arranged plates.

Finally, one of the preeminent controlling factors in what an island looks like today and what lives and grows on it is the presence and activities of humanity. For hundreds of years people and their agriculture, their fires, and their livestock have changed and eliminated vegetation and the soils that support it. Because this changes the "albedo" or solar energy absorption-reflection ratios, it changes climate and rainfall patterns. The result has been "desertification" in many areas of the world. On such small land masses as are described in this account, these events occur rapidly.

In the Lesser Antilles, North Africa, and the Middle East a major factor is the presence of goats. In the Antilles, a climax vegetation type called "goat land" is composed of hurricane grass, croton, physicnut, and other toxic weeds. The propensity of goats to consume everything except the most toxic or nutritionally poor plants results in a characteristic landscape without a bite of fodder for other species.

THE
CAYS

Boat view from the east

Sea grape flowers

Laughing gull

Opposite:
Aerial view from the west

Oystercatcher
One of our year-round resident seabirds, it perches conspicuously on shoreline rocks. Pairs seem to be territorial even outside the breeding season, as each of the smaller islands has only one resident pair. They lay 2 or 3 eggs in May in the seashells and gravel just above the high-water mark. After 3 1/2 weeks of incubation, the chicks hatch and are immediately able to run about. They feed on a variety of mollusks and crustaceans but are particularly noted in the Virgin Islands for being able to extract the whelk or top shell (*Cittarium pica*).

BOOBY ROCK

VEGETATIONAL AND FLORAL FEATURES
Covered by grasses and sedges with small clumps of sea grape which is stunted by the wind and the shallow dry soil pockets in which it grows. Vegetation is largely restricted to the summit and sloping western (leeward) side.

FAUNAL FEATURES
Historically, mountain doves, ground doves, brown boobies, roseate terns, bridled terns, and laughing gulls nested here. Rats are present. Since 1975 no brown boobies have been observed nesting. Roseate terns had 7 eggs in 1984 and 7 eggs in June 1987.

GEOLOGICAL FEATURES
Steep and rough exposed rock on the eastern side, sloping to the splash zone on the west. Soil type Vr.

NEAR SHORE FEATURES
Shallow to the north and east with deeper water on the other side. Provides interesting snorkeling and diving for experienced swimmers.

MANMADE FEATURES
No structures exist, but it has traditionally been "egged" and picked for whelks.

RECOMMENDATIONS
Should be protected as a "no-entry" wildlife management area since its small size precludes any recreational onshore activities.

Booby Rock
- **Location** 18° 18' 15.17" N
  64° 42' 37.28" W
  One-half mile northwest of Ram Head, south of St. John Island.
- **Owner** V.I. Government
- **Acres** .51 (.21 ha)
- **Elevation** 35 ft. (10.67 m)
- **Shoreline** 150 yds. (137 m)

Aerial view from the west

Opposite:
Panorama from the north

Little blue heron

Grass anole
This slender, long-tailed animal is known as the "grass-lizard" because it is nearly always observed on bunches of Guinea grass or thickly spaced vertical tan-tan seedlings. It is unable to mask the bright yellow lateral lines and attempts to avoid detection by keeping a stem between the observer and itself in the manner of many arboreal animals.

Buttonwood fruit

Red mangrove prop roots

BOVONI CAY

Island of mangrove and swamp, 3/4 mile long, with a 75-foot knoll or humpel near the northern end, separating Mangrove Lagoon from Jersey Bay, southeast portion of St. Thomas Island. Small manglars or mangrove clumps in southeast end of Mangrove Lagoon cover nearly 2 acres more. Patricia Cay covering 33.4 acres, south of Bovoni Cay, from which it is separated by a narrow tortuous passage, is of a similar formation, with a knoll of equal height, and has sometimes been considered as a portion of the Bovoni Bay or Cays.

VEGETATIONAL AND FLORAL FEATURES
Fringed by red mangrove which in places is many yards wide. The areas of the cay not affected by the tidal action are covered with croton-acacia scrub mixed with very small areas of dry forest with cactus. An opening in the mangroves of the southern tip creates a hidden "lagoon" that is virtually inaccessible.

FAUNAL FEATURES
Because of Bovoni's proximity to mainland St. Thomas and the shallow intervening waters, much of the St. Thomas fauna is indigenous to the cay. Deer swim back and forth, as do iguanas. Many birds nest in the mangroves and on the higher land. These include great blue heron, great egret, snowy egret, little blue heron, green heron, clapper rail, Wilson's plover, mountain dove, ground dove, white-crowned pigeon, hummingbirds, gray kingbird, vireo, bananaquit, grassquit, and presumably others. The whistling frog, dwarf gecko, house gecko, crested anole, barred anole, grass anole, and common ground lizard have been found.

GEOLOGICAL FEATURES
The higher portions are the tips of low-lying hills with their slopes and bases covered by alluvial fill from mainland St. Thomas. The alluvium has been increased by the deposition of calcareous reef sand along the eastern side. This sand forms a small beach at one point. The land mass and its mangroves separate the "outer" lagoon and open sea from the true inner lagoon lying between the western edge and mainland St. Thomas. Soil types of higher areas are CrE and JuB. These are surrounded by Ts.

NEAR SHORE FEATURES
The northern and southern tips are in contact with channels containing clear tidal water. The shallow seaward flats on the east are covered with turtle grass beds in clear tidal water. The inner lagoon to the west is covered by a grass-algae flat typical of more turbid waters with higher temperatures and salinities.

MANMADE FEATURES
At one time the cay was inhabited and had permanent dwellings. The mangroves have historically been cut for boat building and fuel. Today it is sometimes used illegally by squatters.

RECOMMENDATIONS
Cay and its environs should become a part of the Territorial Park System as the sole remaining example of the lagoon-type habitat in the American Virgin Islands.

Bovoni Cay
Location 18° 18' 50" N
            64° 52' 22" W
Owner   Private
Acres   49.9 (22.3 ha)
Elevation 75 ft. (23 m)
Shoreline 2.3 mi (3.7 km)

NEAR ST. CROIX

Green turtle
The meat of the green turtle has been highly esteemed for centuries. With increased demand, the harvest of turtles and eggs reduced the population to the edge of extinction by 1980. With full protection, the population has recovered to the point that many young turtles can be observed feeding on the seagrass beds in shallow bays in the Virgin Islands.

Cliff orchid

Magnificent frigatebird (male) with inflated throat pouch

Boat view from the south

Lignum vitae

Cotton ginner gecko
This little gecko is found only on St. Croix and its satellite cays.

Opposite:
Aerial from the west

BUCK ISLAND

VEGETATIONAL AND FLORAL FEATURES
Originally covered with a forest of lignum vitae which was removed for commercial purposes and to establish a plantation in 1754. Since the mid-19th century it has recovered to the status of a tropical dry forest with frangipani, cactus and turpentine trees. Many trees are above 20 feet tall. On the northwest and southeast are large open manchineel forests and on the western end coconut palms have been planted near a picnic area.

FAUNAL FEATURES
Most mainland birds can be seen here, and a brown pelican rookery is located on the northeastern end. It is in use from June through March. Magnificent frigatebirds roost here. The St. Croix anole, cotton ginner gecko, and rats are common. This and Sandy Point, St. Croix, are the only recorded locations for green turtle nesting in the U.S. Virgin Islands. Leatherback and hawksbill turtles seasonally nest in numbers. Repeated attempts have been made to eliminate a small population of introduced mongooses.

GEOLOGICAL FEATURES
Most of the higher part of the island has soil type SrF, while bordering this in pockets in the south and west are SaC, outside of which are JuB, one small Tf (tidal flat), and a small salt pond. The western side has a beautiful white coral-sand beach. The gut on the northwest corner has an intermittent stream which was supported by a permanent spring when the original vegetation and soil were present.

NEAR SHORE FEATURES
Most of the island is surrounded by a well-developed coral barrier reef which attracts many snorkelers.

MANMADE FEATURES
The earliest features are two Indian mounds on the northwest shore. The ruins of the plantation run by Dietricks, the Christiansted town clerk in the 1750s, are on the crest of the west ridge. This was followed in time by the ruins of a Danish signal station operated on the highest peak in the late 1700s and early 1800s. Adjoining these ruins is a steel tower with an automatic signal light (flashes every 4 seconds) operated by the Coast Guard. There are permanent moorings and an interpretive snorkel trail inside the reef at the east end, and a cement pier on the south side and picnic areas on the west end.

RECOMMENDATION
Retain as is and reestablish the St. Croix lizard.

Buck Island
(Near St. Croix)
- **Location** 17° 47' 10" N
  64° 37' 00" W
- **Owner** A National Monument administered by the U.S. Government
- **Acres** 179.6 (72.68 ha)
- **Elevation** 360 ft. (109.7 m)
- **Shoreline** 2.5 mi. (4.02 km)

NEAR ST. THOMAS

Wind-pruned Acacia scrub

Puerto Rican racer

Grassy savanna

Aerial from the east of Buck and Capella

Opposite:
Aerial from the east

Sailboat anchorage

BUCK ISLAND

VEGETATIONAL AND FLORAL FEATURES
The original woody canopy was removed long ago. The remaining wood vegetation is wind-flattened scrub and cactus. Much of the island is now covered with grasses and sedges which are maintained by burning and the action of the wind.

FAUNAL FEATURES
Established as the U. S. Buck Island National Wildlife Refuge in 1969 by transfer from the control of the United States Navy to the U.S. Fish and Wildlife Service. Zenaida doves and common ground doves nest here. Rats, crested anoles, slipperyback skinks, and dwarf geckos are all common. The island is the type locality of the Puerto Rican racer, which is restricted to this island and nearby Capella. Red-billed tropicbirds nest at several locations.

GEOLOGICAL FEATURES
Steep exposed cliffs of igneous rock (soil type Vr) appear on all but the north shore and western bay. The highest points are soil type SgE with lower slopes of SgF. The bay area is JuB. A dike with quartz crystals is exposed on the east end.

NEAR SHORE FEATURES
The south shore has relatively deep waters abutting it, while all the other shorelines are surrounded by reef or turtle grass beds. The wreck of the *Wye*, sister ship of the *HMS Rhone*, lies in 5 to 20 ft. of water in the southern bay. A wrecked freighter (*Cartanza*) was recently emplaced in the western bay as a snorkeling and diving site.

MANMADE FEATURES
A navigation light extending 136 feet above low water and a ruined lighthouse-keeper's dwelling are present.

RECOMMENDATIONS
It lends itself well to its present multipurpose usage as a game reserve and recreation site. It is a favorite spot for several forms of outdoor recreation. The operation of submarines for tourist viewing of the adjacent coral gardens is a nonconsumptive use to be encouraged.

Buck Island
(Near St. Thomas)

- **Location**: 18° 16' 45" N
  64° 53' 40" W
- **Owner**: U.S. Government - National Wildlife Refuge
- **Acres**: 41.5 (16.81 ha)
- **Elevation**: 125 ft. (38.1 m)
- **Shoreline**: 2.1 mi (3.37 km)

Pools with boulders

Opposite:
Aerial from the south

Shoreline from the west

Red-billed tropicbird with chick
Rarely seen except when flying, the tropicbird is conspicuous with its long streamer tail, brilliant red beak, and black markings on a white plumage. When pairs are flying together they may utter a ululating shriek which can be heard for a long distance. They lay a single egg in a rock crevice and incubate about 43 days. The chick is able to fly at 3 to 4 months of age. They feed primarily on squid, which are often captured by plunge diving at twilight.

CAPELLA ISLAND

Vegetational and Floral Features
Cactus woodland, dry forest with gumbo limbo, frangipani, mampo, and wind-flattened scrub comprise the woody vegetation. Sea purslane, bay cedar, and sea lavender are found on the beach.

Faunal Features
Red-billed tropicbirds nest in the southeast cliffs, and the salt pond at the bottom of the north-facing slope is utilized as a breeding area by the white-cheeked pintail duck. The endemic Puerto Rican racer is found here as well as on neighboring Buck Island. The crested anole and slipperyback skink are regularly observed lizards. Rats are abundant.

Geological Features
Steep rocky cliffs of igneous rock form the eastern and southern shores (soil type Vr) while the rest of the island slopes to the north with soil types SgE and SgF above the salt pond. Soil type JuB separates the salt pond from the sea.

Near Shore Features
The waters near the north shore cover a well-developed coral reef and offer a fine place for snorkeling. All other waters are much deeper and useful for experienced divers only since they are exposed to the open sea. A huge old anchor chain rests half overgrown with coral off the northeast rocky point.

Manmade Features
None except for the posted wildlife management area signs.

Recommendations
Remain as a game management area and the compatible use as a passive recreation area.

Capella Island

Location	18° 16' 48" N
	65° 53' 35" W
Owner	U.S. Government
	National Wildlife Refuge
Acres	21.97 (8.89 ha)
Elevation	121 ft. (36.88 m)
Shoreline	1.8 mi (2.9 km)

Boat view from the south

Tropicbird flying

Brown noddy tern
Noddy terns arrive on their cliff face nest sites in May and deposit their single egg on small rock ledges. They may also build rudimentary stick nests in low trees and cactus or more rarely on the ground beneath trees. The eggs hatch after 35 days of incubation, and the young develop for about 7 weeks before flying. Due to renesting or late nesting, eggs may be found as late as August. It is not uncommon to have noddys remain in the Virgin Islands until the end of November. They feed on small herring and jacks.

Undercut shoreline on the north

Opposite:
Aerial from the south

30

CARVAL ROCK

VEGETATIONAL AND FLORAL FEATURES
The woody vegetation consists of two small wind-pruned fig trees high on the eastern face. Herbaceaus strand vegetation such as sea purslane sometimes gets a temporary start in crevices lower down.

FAUNAL FEATURES
The cay has no permanent residents, but it is widely used as a roost by seabirds and ospreys. Red-bill tropicbirds, noddy terns, and Zenaida doves nest on its ledge.

GEOLOGICAL FEATURES
Exposed fractured and eroded limestone with varied shapes and balanced "boulders." These rocks are covered with guano but no soil is found other than small amounts of debris trapped in crevices. At times in winter the heavy ground seas shoot up the north face higher than the island.

NEAR SHORE FEATURES
Near the southern base is a shallow coral reef, but the eastern and northern sides have 80 to 90 feet of water within a few feet of the base. An underwater ridge extends westward toward Congo. Used constantly as a dive site by tour operators.

MANMADE FEATURES
None.

RECOMMENDATIONS
Retain as a single purpose, "no-entry" wildlife management area since it is unsafe to go ashore.

Carval Rock

Location	18° 22' 18" N
	64° 47' 41" W
Owner	V. I. Government
Acres	.403 (.163 ha)
Elevation	67 ft. (20.4 m)
Shoreline	0.1 mi (.16 km)

Judy Pierce

White-tailed tropicbird
The white-tailed tropicbird breeds in the Virgin Islands in winter and spring. It nests in small caves and rock crevices on sea cliffs where both parents share incubation and feeding duties for the 3-month incubation and development period. Feeding is by plunge diving for small fish and squid or by capturing flying fish while airborn. When the sea is calm they may alight and float delicately with highly arched tail.

Boat view of the cliffs from the south

Red mangrove flowers

Grass orchid

Hydrothermal rock outcrop

Opposite: Aerial view from the west

CAS CAY

Vegetational and Floral Features
The highest elevations on the eastern, windward point are covered with grasses and sedges. The grass orchid can be found in rock crevices. The leeward areas are covered by dry forest, including mampo, sea grape, and inkberry, which merges with a fringing stand of red mangrove.

Faunal Features
The white-cheeked pintail, and red-billed and white-tailed tropicbirds nest on the exposed eastern and southern sides. Roseate terns historically nested on the cliffs. The local egret and heron species are found here year-round, and most of them have nested on the cay. Deer are transient. The crested anole, slippery-backed skink, common ground lizard, dwarf gecko, and iguana are present. The Puerto Rican racer, rats, and mice are abundant on the cay. Domestic animals have used it for grazing.

Geological Features
The seaward sides are very steeply sloping (Vr) soil types. In one spot these display an array of mauve pink and white where the oxidized surfaces were blasted away during the filming of a motion picture. The leeward side of Red Point has soil type CrF while the western slope is JuB.

Near Shore Features
The leeward (northern) or lagoon side abuts a shallow turtle grass-covered sand bottom. The seaward side of Red Point (eastern end) has deeper water close to the shore with extensive spur and groove coral formations. Off the western tip is a narrow deep channel with a sand bottom, and just outside this along the south and west sides is an extensive "flat" which is often exposed at low tides and is being colonized by red mangrove.

Recommendations
This cay along with Bovoni and Patricia should become part of the Virgin Islands Park System as protection for the entire lagoon area. It is an ideal cay for multipurpose recreational, wildlife refuge use.

Cas Cay

Location	18° 18' 30" N
	64° 51' 58" W
Owner	V. I. Government
Acres	14.84 (6.0 ha)
Elevation	99 ft. (30 m)
Shoreline	0.8 mi (1.29 km)

Tilted rock strata

Acacia flowers

Dwarf Gecko

Geckos

The family Geckonidae is worldwide in distribution, ranging from tropical rain forest to temperate deserts. The world's smallest lizard is a gecko from the British Virgin Islands, and some others reach upwards of a foot in length. Many have toe pads that allow them to run across smooth ceilings and panes of glass. Many, but not all, lack eyelids that close and have instead a clear scale, like that of snakes, that covers the eye. They are the only lizards with a voice; they can squeak and "bark." Most are nocturnal and appear at dusk or after dark, but some are active during the day. The American Virgin Islands have 3 native species of gecko and 1 which has been introduced from Africa, probably as a hitchhiker on slave ships. The 2 smallest species, the dwarf gecko and the St. Croix gecko, are very numerous in leaf litter and other ground debris. All geckos feed on insects and other arthropods, with the sizes of prey matching the size of the lizard. The African house gecko often seen feeding near lights at night is a communal nester, as are a number of other gecko species. Several females deposit round, hard-shelled, pea-sized, white eggs in dark dry corners, sometimes even in dresser drawers! At times a dozen or so eggs are found in one of these clutches with some empty, hatched shells and some still developing.

Opposite:
Aerial view from the southeast

CINNAMON CAY

Islet 150 yards long covered with tall grass and cactus, 230 yards from beach at Cinnamon Bay, north shore of St. John.

VEGETATIONAL AND FLORAL FEATURES
Guinea grass and maran are interspersed with frangipani, wild tamarind, *Acacia*, tree cacti, and sea grape.

FAUNAL FEATURES
Common ground doves, Zenaida doves, and gray kingbirds are known to nest here. The crested anole and dwarf gecko are present, as are rats.

GEOLOGICAL FEATURES
The cay has rocky shorelines composed of steeply tilted beds of conglomerate on the seaward side. The inland side is more gently sloping. Soil type is Vr.

NEAR SHORE FEATURES
A shoal extends from the point nearest shore to Cinnamon Bay Beach. This provides protected snorkeling for beginners.

MANMADE FEATURES
None.

RECOMMENDATIONS
Should be acquired by the National Park Service.

Cinnamon Cay

Location	18° 21' 30" N
	64° 45' 2" W
Owner	Private
Acres	1.027 (.415 ha)
Elevation	32 ft. (9.75 m)
Shoreline	.2 mi (.32 km)

Lens-shaped boulders

Masked booby
The strikingly marked masked booby is seldom seen except near Cockroach Island and the deep waters north of St. Thomas. They lay 2 eggs on the ground in the fall or winter but raise only one chick, which flies at about 120 days of age. Their diet is composed of flying fish and other surface-feeding pelagic fish, such as halfbeaks. The sexes appear similar, but females honk and males whistle.

Crab bush flower

Opposite:
Aerial view from the south

Common sedge

Boat view from the east

COCKROACH CAY

Island 500 yards long 3 1/4 miles north-northwest of western end of St. Thomas Island, and 2,700 yards north of Dutchcap Cay. Also called "Big Cockroach," in distinction from Cricket Cay, formerly called "Little Cockroach." Also called *La Isla Cockroach*, or *El Islote Cockroach*. Spanish equivalent, *Cayo Cucaracha*; Danish, *Kakerlak*. Another islet, in British Virgin Islands, Lat. 18° x 30' 10", Long. 64° x 27' 44" is also called "Cockroach."

VEGETATIONAL AND FLORAL FEATURES
The dominant vegetation is the common sedge and the spiney shrub, locally called crab bush. A few sea grape and fig trees are found in crevices along the cliffs and near jumbles of rock. This vegetational structure has probably been maintained largely by fire since "the roach" has been repeatedly burned to produce pasture.

FAUNAL FEATURES
The most notable animal here is the masked booby. Aside from Monito Island, Puerto Rico, this is the only known breeding colony of these birds in United States territory. The brown booby also nests here as do the red-billed tropicbird, white-tailed tropicbird, Audubon's shearwater, bridled tern, laughing gull, and noddy tern. Zenaida doves and other terrestrial species also utilize the island. The crested anole and dwarf gecko are recorded along with the Puerto Rican racer.

GEOLOGICAL FEATURES
There are steep, fractured cliffs on all sides except the northeast corner where a flat shield slopes into the water. At both the east and west ends, the tips of the island have tilted into the sea leaving smaller masses separated by large crevices. The easternmost of these is known as Sula Cay. Interesting jumbles of boulders are etched against the skyline like a group of praying monks. Soil type CsF is found on the highest ridges in the center. This is surrounded by type Vr.

NEAR SHORE FEATURES
In the pocket near Sula Cay on the south side there is a shallow reef area. On all other sides there is deep water covering masses of huge boulders. This makes dramatic diving; however, strong currents, wave surge, and the probability of sharks make it appropriate for only the more experienced divers.

MANMADE FEATURES
None; however, the north side is used by fishermen when the weather allows access, and, as mentioned above, deliberate burning has occurred over a long period of time.

RECOMMENDATIONS
Protect as an inviolate, "no-entry" seabird breeding area.

Cockroach Cay
Location 18° 24' 15" N
65° 03' 48" N
Owner V. I. Government
Acres 19.039 (7.7 ha)
Elevation 151 ft. (46 m)
Shoreline 1 mi (1.6 km)

Boat view from the east

A.E. Dammann

Crested anole
This is the largest member of the genus in the northern Virgin Islands, and the sexes are quite distinct. Mature males have a dorsal vertebral "sail" as well as another on the tail. Males have an extensive array of body patterns and shades of color. Bars, blotches, and net-like reticulations appear and disappear in shades of grey and brown from pale to dark chocolate. The female is much smaller, lacks the dorsal crests, and retains a yellowish vertebral stripe. Both sexes are territorial, but the males especially have a ritualized combat in which, with cat-like lashing tails, pushups, and extensions of the gular flap, they attempt to intimidate their opponent. If this fails, they resort to physical combat, in which the objective is to lock jaws in such a manner that one of the combatants is flipped from the perch and loses the encounter.

Buttonwood flowers

Opposite:
Aerial view from the east

Windswept vegetation

Sea grape
The hardy sea grape is one of the few woody plants that grow on windy, salty shorelines. They bear grapelike clusters of fruits which are purple when ripe. The fruit may be eaten fresh or prepared as a jelly or beverage.

COCOLOBA CAY

Steep islet covered with growth of cocolobo or sea grapes, *Coccoloba uvifera*; situated east of Fish Bay, 85 yards from southern shore of St. John Island, to which the cay is joined by a reef 3 feet deep. (Not Fish Cay.)

VEGETATIONAL AND FLORAL FEATURES
The crown is covered by wind-pruned buttonwood, sea grape, and turskcap cacti. Sea purslane and leatherleaf are found at low elevation where wave action and salt spray limit the distribution of woody plants. A coconut tree is in a pocket of soil on the west side.

FAUNAL FEATURES
Many species of birds utilize this small cay because of its relative isolation. Roseate terns historically nested here and ground doves presently nest here. Rats are present along with the crested anole and dwarf gecko.

GEOLOGICAL FEATURES
This is the tip of a nearshore "rock" that is separated from St. John by a narrow shoal. It is composed of conglomerates and other metamorphic rocks intruded by dikes. Soil type is Vr.

NEAR SHORE FEATURES
A breaking reef reaches from the eastern edge of the cay to the mainland while a sand and finger coral shoal covers the area between the cay and shore. In calm weather there is good and interesting snorkeling and diving in the area.

MANMADE FEATURES
None.

RECOMMENDATIONS
Maintain in an undisturbed state as part of Virgin Islands National Park.

Cocoloba Cay
Location	18° 19' 02" N
	64° 45' 37" W
Owner	U. S. Government
Acres	1.076 (.435 ha)
Elevation	36 ft. (11 m)
Shoreline	.2 mi (.32 km)

Humpback whale
In winter, humpback whales migrate to the warm waters of the Caribbean to mate and calve. They are commonly seen between Outer Brass and Congo Cays and can be distinguished by long white flippers and knobs on top of the head and lower jaw. They typically blow 2 to 4 times before they raise their flukes clear of the water to commence a long dive. Humpback whales may be boisterous, leap clear of the water (a 50-foot whale generates a large splash), slap a flipper against the water, or crash the tail onto the water. A slow approach to within a quarter-mile in a small boat allows interesting viewing without disturbing the whale.

Brown pelican nest

Opposite:
Aerial view from the south

Gumbo limbo tree

Boat view from the south

Cliffs from the north

CONGO CAY

Lanceolate or shuttle-shaped island 1,240 yards long, 160 yards wide, 260 yards north of Lovango Cay. Also called "Cam Island," *Kukelusse Kay* (variants *Kukkelusse, Cucculus, Coculus*); *El Cayo Congo o Lovango Chico*, or simply *Lovango Chico*. The eastern extremity is called "Indian Inscription Point," because of the petroglyphs found there.

VEGETATIONAL AND FLORAL FEATURES
A closed-canopy dry forest with the trees growing from the jumble of marble boulders that comprises the mass of the island. Sea grapes line the shores above the splash zone while fig and gumbo limbo trees grow to a fair size.

FAUNAL FEATURES
Red-billed and white-tailed tropicbirds, bridled terns, noddy terns and Zenaida doves utilize the area for nesting. It is a major nesting site for the endangered brown pelican, which nests in the treetops on the northern cliffs. However, high wintertime surge sometimes destroys nests along with eggs and young birds. Goats were introduced but are now eliminated. The crested anole, barred anole, and dwarf gecko occur along with the Puerto Rican racer, rats, and mice. Humpback whales are commonly seen north of the island in the winter.

GEOLOGICAL FEATURES
This is an extremely rocky, jumbled landscape primarily of marble. The seaward side (in this case the northern one) drops steeply into deep water. Wave action has produced undercuts at the base of the cliffs. However, even on the less steep southern side large boulders extend to the waterline. Banded onyx can be found in old cracks in the marble.

NEAR SHORE FEATURES
There is deep water on the north and a sandy shoal with coral heads on the south between this cay and Lovango. There is good snorkeling, but a swift current runs at tidal changes. Dive tour operators use near shore waters daily.

MANMADE FEATURES
On the extreme eastern end are interesting rock carvings (Indian?) which are weathering badly and nearly hidden by guano. Pottery shards have been found. It has been used for grazing but is unsuited for development.

RECOMMENDATIONS
Retain as a protected brown pelican nesting sanctuary. A proposed plan to reintroduce the endangered St. Thomas tree boa should proceed.

Congo Cay
- **Location** 18° 22' 22" N, 64° 48' 10" W
- **Owner** V. I. Government
- **Acres** 25.46 (10.6 ha)
- **Elevation** 170 ft. (51.8 m)
- **Shoreline** 1.6 mi (2.57 km)

Boat view from the east

Bridled tern
The adult bridled terns return to the Virgin Islands in late April and select their solitary nest sites from rock crevices. A single egg is deposited in May. The 29-day incubation period is followed by 55 days of development. Bridled terns feed on small fish and squid taken by plunging into the water. They do swim on occasion. They usually leave the Virgin Islands by the end of September.

Opposite:
Aerial view from the south

Sea purslane flower

Brown booby

CRICKET ROCK

Steep pinnacled islet, over 1,000 yards east-northeast from Cockroach Island and 3 1/2 miles north of west end St. Thomas. Also called "Cricket," *La Roca Cricket,* "Little Cockroach." The equivalents, *Grillo* (Spanish) and *Faarakyllying* (Danish) not on charts.

VEGETATIONAL AND FLORAL FEATURES

There are a few sedge and grass clumps in the most protected areas. Heavy surge and spray prohibit the growth of woody plants. Sea purslane is present in soil pockets at higher elevations.

FAUNAL FEATURES

Masked boobies may sometimes nest here. Brown booby, roseate tern, bridled tern, red-billed tropicbird, brown noddy, and Zenaida doves nest regularly.

GEOLOGICAL FEATURES

An exposed and tilted rock mass of soil type Vr.

NEAR SHORE FEATURES

Deep water surrounds the cay, with a narrow submerged rock ledge off the southeast point.

MANMADE FEATURES

None, except military ammunition fragments.

RECOMMENDATIONS

Maintain as a "no-entry" bird sanctuary.

Cricket Rock

Location	18° 21' 17" N
	65° 03' 52" W
Owner	V. I. Government
Acres	2.520 (1.02 ha)
Elevation	46 ft. (14.0 m)
Shoreline	525 yds. (.48 km)

Boat view from the south

Dildo Cactus

Opposite:
Aerial view from the north

Rocky shoreline

Laughing gull nest

Laughing gull
The laughing gull is abundant throughout the Virgin Islands in the summer months. The first arrivals of the season are usually in late March. They nest on many of the cays, where they lay 2 or 3 grey-green spotted eggs. After an incubation period of 27 days, the young fledge at about 40 days of age. The adults are scavengers, eating live fish, carrion, crabs, insects, and other birds' eggs.

CURRENT ROCK

Islet, area 65 square yards, in middle of Current Hole, off east end of St. Thomas. *Schorbomonoch Eyland* of Van Keulen's map seems to be identical with this, though *Schorbomonok Isle*, of Bellin's atlas, (evidently same name) may be Steven Cay.

VEGETATIONAL AND FLORAL FEATURES
Low, wind-flattened sea grape and buttonwood, with interspersed dildo and turskcap cactus.

Current Rock

Location	18° 19' 00" N
	64° 50' 01" W
Owner	Private
Acres	.404 (.16 ha)
Elevation	13 ft. (4.0 m)
Shoreline	100 yds (.09 km)

FAUNAL FEATURES
The crested anole has been collected, and rats have been seen. Zenaida doves, oystercatchers, and laughing gulls sometimes nest here. Many seabirds rest and fish from this small cay. Deer swimming between St. Thomas and Great St. James often stop here.

GEOLOGICAL FEATURES
Soil type is Vr. A very low "rock" emerging between St. Thomas and Great St. James.

NEAR SHORE FEATURES
Surrounded by very shallow waters with a channel eight feet deep on the west between the light and St. Thomas. A channel with a 20-foot depth occurs on the east between the light and Great St. James. Strong reversing tidal currents in the surrounding water give the rock its name.

MANMADE FEATURES
A flashing, red, 6-second, 20-foot navigation light is installed at the north end.

RECOMMENDATIONS
Maintain in its present condition.

Boat view from the south

Bromeliad

Turkscap cactus group

Woolly nipple cactus
A rounded cactus, often growing in clusters of up to 25 heads. The spine areoles are woolly when young. The red fruit is edible. Collecting of this cactus from the wild is rendering it increasingly scarce. The type locality from which it was first described is Tortola.

Opposite:
Aerial view
from the east

DOG ISLAND

One-fourth mile long, 1/4 mile east-southeast of Little St. James Island. So named on all modern charts. Called by the Dutch and Danes *Hund* or *Hunde Eyland*; by the Creoles, *Hond*; and by the Spanish, *Isla del Perro*.

VEGETATIONAL AND FLORAL FEATURES
Turkshead and woolly nipple cactus and clumps of terrestrial bromeliads abound. Black mangrove surrounds the salt pond.

FAUNAL FEATURES
The white-tailed tropicbird, white-cheeked pintail duck, laughing gull, roseate tern, sooty tern, bridled tern, ground dove, and Zenaida dove nest here. The crested anole, dwarf gecko and the Puerto Rican racer are also found here. Deer and rats are seen here, and hawksbill turtles nest on the beach.

GEOLOGICAL FEATURES
The metamorphic rock is intruded by many dikes, some with quartz crystals. There is a tiny, secluded sand beach on the northwest tip and a crescent-shaped salt pond.

NEAR SHORE FEATURES
A beautiful reef at the west end provides good snorkeling for experienced swimmers. Dog rocks is a line of isolated rocks extending to the east. The wreck of a self-powered barge, the *Daisy*, lies in shallow water to the east of a line of rocks extending to the south.

MANMADE FEATURES
None.

RECOMMENDATIONS
Should be incorporated into the V. I. park system with entry prohibited during the nesting period.

Dog Island
- **Location** 18° 17' 52" N
  64° 49' 00" W
- **Owner** V. I. Government
- **Acres** 12.137 (4.91 ha)
- **Elevation** 78 ft. (23.77 m)
- **Shoreline** .9 mi (1.45 km)

Magnificent frigatebird (female) with fish

Frigatebirds are year-round residents of the Virgin Islands. They nest in colonies, building their twig nests in low trees or cactus. The single egg is incubated for 54 days, and the young develop for an additional 24 weeks before flying. After the young birds fly, they return to the nest for supplemental feeding by parents for 6 to 10 months. Excellent and acrobatic fliers, their feathers are not waterproof. They gather all their food while flying, either stealing it from other seabirds or snatching fish from near the surface of the sea. The inflated red throat pouch is a territorial display by breeding males. The females have white heads.

Nesting group of red-footed boobies

Tree cactus

White phase red-footed booby on nest

Boat view from the south

Opposite:
Aerial view from the east

DUTCHCAP CAY

Dome-shaped rocky islet, 600 yards long, 1 mile north-northwest of Salt Cay and 2 miles off Botany Point, St. Thomas. Channel to north named Dutchcap Passage. On most charts the cay is called "Dutchman's Cap," "Dutchman Cap," or "Dutchmancap"; also called *Gorro Flamenco* (Flemish Cap).

VEGETATIONAL AND FLORAL FEATURES
A forest of prickly pear tree cactus on the east and southeast sides, an open park-like fig forest on the north, and *Acacia* and crab bush on the south.

FAUNAL FEATURES
A large colony (200 pairs) of pelicans nest here. The red-footed booby (100 pairs), brown booby (500 pairs), red-billed and white-tailed tropicbirds, and noddy and bridled terns also nest here. The common ground lizard and crested anole are found here, along with rats. Historically both masked boobies and frigatebirds have been reported as nesting. Introduced goats have been eliminated.

GEOLOGICAL FEATURES
There are detached rocks on the southwest tip. Steep and ruggedly beautiful cliffs of layered sedimentary rock are on the north and east faces. Soil type Vr rings the island while a large area of CsF is found on the higher elevations.

NEAR SHORE FEATURES
The shore drops steeply to depths of 100 feet on all sides. Strong currents are present on all sides.

MANMADE FEATURES
None.

RECOMMENDATIONS
Should be a "no-entry" sanctuary.

Dutchcap Cay
- **Location** 18° 22' 55" N 65° 03' 35" W
- **Owner** V. I. Government
- **Acres** 31.82 (12.87 ha)
- **Elevation** 278 ft. (84.0 m)
- **Shoreline** 1800 yds (1.64 km)

Samphire flower

Boat view from the north

Acacia bush

Pelican

Opposite;
Aerial view from the north

A. E. Dammann

Male crested anole

The anoles are a very large genus of about 300 species in the family Iguanidae. Members occur throughout the American tropics, but only 4 species are resident in the U.S. Virgin Islands. The St. Croix anole is restricted to St. Croix and its cays. The 3 species are often found in close proximity to one another but have very different habits and appearance. The crested anole (on trees near the ground), barred anole (in the upper tree branches), and grass anole (on guinea grass near brush) are found on St. Thomas, St. John, and surrounding cays. They are all primarily carnivorous and feed on a variety of insects and arachnids. Some, particularly the crested anole, eat some plant material and learn to feed from pet-food dishes. All mate and reproduce year-round and are very territorial.

FISH CAY

Islet with 2 adjacent boulders in St. James Bay, 300 yards west of Great St. James Island.

VEGETATIONAL AND FLORAL FEATURES
The vegetation on the upper part of the island is sea grape, *Acacia*, buttonwood, haiti-haiti, and sedge.

FAUNAL FEATURES
Zenaida doves, common ground doves, and other birds utilize it for resting and fishing. The crested anole has been collected, and the house gecko has been recorded.

Fish Cay
Location 18° 18' 40" N
64° 50' 02" W
Owner Private
Acres .351 (.14 ha)
Elevation 21 ft. (6.4 m)
Shoreline .1 mi (.16 km)

GEOLOGICAL FEATURES
There is a sandy beach on the east side. Soil type Vr makes up the rest of the key.

NEAR SHORE FEATURES
There is good snorkeling - the eastern tip with a very shoal sandy flat, and deeper water with soft coral and sponges on the west.

MANMADE FEATURES
None.

RECOMMENDATIONS
Private but probably too small for development. Highly valued as an interest spot for yachts which heavily utilize Christmas Cove as anchorage. Should be acquired by the V. I. Government as an addition to the territorial park system.

Boat view from the south

Leatherleaf flower

Roseate tern group
Roseate terns return to the Virgin Islands each year in late April but usually don't select an Island and aggregate as a colony until late May. They frequently choose different small islands for nesting each year. They are very sensitive and will abandon a nesting colony if disturbed.

Cactus-covered cliff on the east

Opposite:
Aerial view from the east

FLANAGAN ISLAND

This island is .75 mile southeast of Privateer Point, St. John Island. A rock at west has an area of .32 acres, height 45 feet. Also called "Flemingham Cay," and by the Spanish, *Cayo Consejos*.

VEGETATIONAL AND FLORAL FEATURES
On the east side there is windswept scrub and prickly pear cactus. There is canopied vegetation on the western side in the lee. Many frangipani are present.

FAUNAL FEATURES
A roseate tern colony occupies the rocks on the southwest side along with bridled terns and laughing gulls. Zenaida doves nest in the rocks and forest. The common ground lizard, crested anole, barred anole, and dwarf gecko inhabit the island. A group of smooth-billed anis appears to be resident on the island.

GEOLOGICAL FEATURES
There are cliffs on the southwest end showing the intrusion and engulfing of darker igneous rocks by lighter quartz-containing rocks. A rubble beach allows an easy protected landing on the west side. Soil type is Vr.

NEAR SHORE FEATURES
The western bay provides excellent snorkeling with clear protected water and interesting coral.

MANMADE FEATURES
The tern rookery has been traditionally disturbed for egg harvesting. Many fishermen use it as a resting or overnight spot.

RECOMMENDATIONS
Retain as a wildlife sanctuary.

Flanagan Island

Location	18° 19' 45" N
	64° 49' 00" W
Owner	V.I. Government
Acres	21.618 (8.74 ha)
Elevation	127 ft. (38.7 m)
Shoreline	0.8 mi (1.2 km)

Boat view from the east

Royal tern with sandwich terns
The royal tern is the largest tern found in the Virgin Islands and the only tern found here year-round. In mid-May they lay their large single egg in a depression on the ground. After 30 days of incubation and another 30 days of development, the young fly. The young birds leave the Virgin Islands by September, while some of the adults stay throughout the winter. They feed in flocks on schools of small herrings and anchovies.

Little Flat Cay

Prickly pear tree

Vine-covered upland with nesting terns

Opposite:
Aerial view from the west

Flat Cay

and Little Flat Cay

Two islets, 1.33 miles southwest of Red Point, 7/8 mile northeast of Saba Cay. Big Flat or Raso, the larger, is 220 yards long, 32 feet high, area 2.94 acres; the smaller, Little Flat or Rasito, is 11 feet high, 57 yards long, area .378 acres; together 3.27 acres. Also called *Plat Eyland, Isle Plate, Los Cayos Rasos*, Flatkeys.

Vegetational and Floral Features
The vegetation is dominated by prickly pear cactus, sedges, and vines.

Faunal Features
Zenaida doves, common ground doves, white-cheeked pintail ducks, bridled terns, laughing gulls, royal, sooty, roseate, and sandwich terns, oystercatchers, red-billed tropicbirds, and brown noddies nest here. The crested anole, common ground lizard, and dwarf gecko are found on Big Flat Cay.

Geological Features
The Vr soil type slopes from 30-foot cliffs on the west to a rubble beach on the east. Potholes sometimes hold rainwater. A sand beach is present on the northeast corner of Big Flat Cay.

Near Shore Features
There is an extensive shallow reef to the east while the other sides drop off to a depth of about 40 feet.

Manmade Features
None.

Recommendations
Should be protected as a "no-entry" wildlife sanctuary.

Flat Cay
Little Flat Cay

- **Location** 18° 19' 08" N
  64° 59' 25" W
- **Owner** V. I. Government
- **Acres** 2.894 (1.17 ha)
  .378 (.152 ha)
- **Elevation** 32 ft. (9.7 m)
  11 ft. (3.3 m)
- **Shoreline** 1900 ft. (0.579 km)

Red-footed booby with chick
The red-footed booby in the Virgin Islands occurs as two distinct but freely interbreeding forms. The white form is white with black primary and secondary feathers. The brown form is overall brown with a white tail and rump. Both phases have brilliant red feet. They build twig nests on the tops of fig and several other species of trees. A single egg is incubated for 45 days before hatching. The chick becomes quite agile and moves about in the branches near the nest until it first flies at about 100 days of age. The parents continue to feed the chick for an additional 3 months as it learns to forage. They feed on squid and flying fish, often catching flying fish while the fish are in the air.

Peregrine falcon

Red-footed booby (brown form)

Wind-pruned fig

Opposite: Aerial view from the east

Frenchcap Cay

Steep, rocky, grass-covered islet, 200 by 300 yards in size, 3.5 miles southeast of Capella Islands, 5 miles south of east end of St. Thomas, and 4.3 miles 208° from Dog Island. By Danish called *Fugleklippen*; French, *Islet Rond* or *Caye des Oiseaux*; Spanish, *Cayo Franced o de Aves*; English, Bird's Key, Round Island, or Frenchman's Cap.

Vegetational and Floral Features

The dominant vegetation is sedge with clumps of wind-sheared fig scattered on the northeast slope. Crab bush and leatherleaf occur at lower elevations with beach pea creeping over bare rock.

Frenchcap Cay
- **Location** 18° 13' 59" N 64° 51' 09" W
- **Owner** V. I. Government
- **Acres** 10.5 (4.2 ha)
- **Elevation** 183 ft. (55.8 m)
- **Shoreline** 700 yds. (.64 km)

Faunal Features

There is a brown booby rookery (500 pairs) here. Brown noddy and bridled terns nest in the western cliffs and under the fig trees. A small colony of sooty terns is established on the lower southwest slope and higher. Laughing gulls nest interspersed among the boobies at higher elevations. A group of red-footed boobies has nested in the ficus trees since 1983. Several pairs of Zenaida doves seem to be resident, and the endangered peregrine falcon is frequently seen. The crested anole and dwarf gecko are present.

Geological Features

The darker gabbro and lighter granite rock produce high cliffs and shallow caves on the west side and southwest corner. The highest elevation is soil type SgE, and surrounding lower regions are Vr.

Near Shore Features

The small western shelf dropping off to deep waters offers good snorkeling to the west and scuba diving to the north and east.

Manmade Features

A U.S.G.S. benchmark is on the peak.

Recommendations

Should become a "no-entry" wildlife sanctuary.

Vertical rock strata

Opposite:
Aerial view from the south

Century plant flower

House gecko
Originally from West Africa, this gecko, also called "woodslave," is widely distributed in the Caribbean. It adapts well to the presence of people and frequently takes refuge by day behind hanging pictures, curtains, or bookcases. It emerges at night to pursue insects attracted by lights to walls and ceilings. One of the few vocal lizards, the "gek-gek-gek" call can be heard by day if the refuge is disturbed and by night as individuals dispute territorial rights to specific sections of walls or ceilings.

Boat view from the north

GRASS CAY

Cay is 1,660 yards long, 75 to 300 yards wide, with shore rocks and ledges attached to Eastend Quarter, St. Thomas. Grass Cay is less than 100 yards west of Mingo Cay, but is separated from Thatch Cay on the west by Middle Passage, 1/2 mile wide. Name spelled also Gras or Graes; also called Green or Grass Kay.

VEGETATIONAL AND FLORAL FEATURES
Patches of dry forest interspersed with maran and *Acacia* cover the island. Tyre palm is present at the higher elevations. Century plants, sea grape, and figs grow on the harsh slopes and cliffs.

Grass Cay
Location	18° 21' 40" N
	64° 50' 00" W
Owner	V. I. Government
Acres	48.77 (19.74 ha)
Elevation	230 ft. (70.1 m)
Shoreline	.3 mi (3.7 km)

FAUNAL FEATURES
Zenaida doves and common ground doves nest on the island. Red-billed tropicbirds nest in the northern cliffs. The crested anole, dwarf gecko, house gecko and Puerto Rican racer are present.

GEOLOGICAL FEATURES
The north and west side exhibit beautiful, vertically-aligned, sedimentary rock formations. The soil types are CsF on the central ridge and Vr at the lower elevations.

NEAR SHORE FEATURES
There is deep water on the north side and shoals to the south. Strong currents sweep both the east and west ends. About 100 yards west of the island, a rock rises out of 70 feet of water to within 3 feet of the surface.

MANMADE FEATURES
None

RECOMMENDATIONS
Should be established as a multipurpose recreation area.

Peregrine falcon

Kestrel

Black-necked stilt

St. Thomas tree boa
The endangered St. Thomas tree boa is smaller than most boas and spends its days hiding in old termite nests or rockpiles. By night it seeks sleeping lizards while slithering through the slim branches of shrubs.

Opposite: Aerial view from the south

GREAT ST. JAMES ISLAND

Length 1 mile, off eastern extremity of St. Thomas Island. The alternative names are all translations: Dutch, *Groot St. Jems*; German, *Gross St. James*; Danish, *Store St. James*; French, *Grand St. James*; Spanish, *Santiago Grande*. Also called simply Saint James Island.

VEGETATIONAL AND FLORAL FEATURES

Manchineel is common in the coves behind the sand beaches and around the salt pond on the southeast peninsula. On the northern peninsula are windswept grass, sedges, and cactus. A well-developed canopy is present behind the large north cove and on the southeast corner behind the peninsula. The vegetation is similar in species composition to nearby St. Thomas.

Great St. James Island

- *Location* 18° 18' 31" N
  64° 49' 55" W
- *Owner* Private
- *Acres* 156.86 (63.48 ha)
- *Elevation* 175 ft. (53.3 m)
- *Shoreline* 3.9 mi (6.27 km)

FAUNAL FEATURES

Many rats and mice are present. The white-cheeked pintail duck nests here and the rest of the St. Thomas bird fauna is probably present. Also present are the crested anole, grass anole, barred anole, dwarf gecko, common ground lizard, St. Thomas worm lizard, and Puerto Rican racer. Hawksbill turtles nest on the beaches. White-tailed deer are permanent residents. The endangered St. Thomas tree boa is on the island.

GEOLOGICAL FEATURES

The geology is complex, with faults, underwater lava flows, beds of volcanic ash, and intrusions. Salt ponds and a jasper outcrop are present. The central area of the island is CsF. There are Vr cliffs and several JuB beach flats.

NEAR SHORE FEATURES

Sandy and protected shoals are present on the west at Christmas Cove, Fish Cay, and two northern bays. There are two shipwrecks off the northeast point in about 40 feet of water.

MANMADE FEATURES

A cotton plantation was in operation here in 1777, and the ruins are still present. The island has been continuously inhabited for more than 20 years and now has a large residence with tennis courts and other amenities.

RECOMMENDATIONS

Government acquisition as a multiple use recreation and wildlife management area. Because of its size and proximity to St. Thomas, it is probable that this cay retains the biota of the larger islands. Sensitive management by the owners offers a chance to preserve that biota.

NEAR ST. CROIX

Snowy egret

Little blue heron

Boat view from the south

Bahama duck

St. Croix ground lizard
The world population of the St. Croix ground lizard exists on Green and Protestant Cays off the north coast of St. Croix. While this small population appears to be stable, a series of severe storms or the introduction of a predator such as the mongoose could result in its extinction.

Opposite: Aerial view from the north

GREEN CAY
ST. CROIX

Islet, 595 yards long, 70 to 150 yards wide, 1,100 yards west of Pull Point, and 1.75 miles east-northeast of Fort Louis Augusta, St. Croix. Cay rises in 2 knolls: southern 55 feet high, northern "Green" knoll, 50 feet high. North and northeast points are clearing marks, leading east of Scotch Bank. French name, *Ile Verte* (confused with Buck Island); Spanish, *Cayo Verde*; Dutch, *Groen Eyland*; German, *Grun Kay*, Danish, *Gron Key*. Also called Little Green Key.

VEGETATIONAL AND FLORAL FEATURES
Prickly pear and dildo cactus grow on the east. Manchineel on the north is wind-sheared and low. Buttonwood mangrove is present on the south slope near the water.

FAUNAL FEATURES

> **Green Cay, St. Croix**
> *Location* 17° 46' 00" N
> 64° 40' 00" W
> *Owner* U. S. Fish and Wildlife Service
> *Acres* 12.77 (5.17 ha)
> *Elevation* 63 ft. (19.2 m)
> *Shoreline* 4500 ft. (1.37 km)

This cay supports the largest of the two populations of the endangered St. Croix ground lizard. Other lizards present are the St. Croix anole, cotton ginner gecko, and slipperyback skink. The cay is used for nesting by great blue herons, snowy egret, little blue heron, tricolor heron, green-backed heron, yellow-crowned night heron, white-cheeked pintail, oystercatcher, and numerous songbirds. At one time, white-crowned pigeons were so numerous that hunters from Puerto Rico and the U.S. mainland made the place famous as a hunting destination.

GEOLOGICAL FEATURES
There is a sandy spit on the southeast tip with shallow caves and a sandy beach on the south shore, and also a small sandy beach on the northwest shore. Soil types are SrF, JuB, and SaC.

NEAR SHORE FEATURES
The east side is protected by a barrier reef. The west side is a protected anchorage under normal wind and sea conditions.

MANMADE FEATURES
A conch shell Indian kitchen midden is present on the east side.

RECOMMENDATIONS
The cay has been purchased by the U. S. Fish and Wildlife Service as a critical habitat for the St. Croix ground lizard and should be maintained as a "no-entry" wildlife preserve.

NEAR ST. THOMAS

Boat view from the west

Frangipani flower

Weathered rock

Wild frangipani
A hardy plant, the wild frangipani is able to grow on steep dry slopes on which the only soil is in rock crevices. The fragrant delicate flowers evoke images of the tropical islands on which they are found. Care should be taken in handling the plant because the milky white sap can cause inflamation of mouth and eye membranes. The frangipani has been widely cultivated, leading to domestic forms with broader leaves and several colors of flowers.

Opposite: Aerial view from the north

Frangipani tree

Green Cay

St. Thomas

Brush islet, 95 yards long, 200 yards off point southeast of French Bay, St. Thomas. Rocks, dry or awash, 13 square rods extend 120 yards southwest from Green Cay. Synonyms are *Groen Yeland, Cayo Verde* in Spanish. Also called simply *Klippen,* "Rocks."

Vegetational and Floral Features

The periphery is occupied by buttonwood and sea grape with the top of the island having a heterogeneous growth composed of prickly pear cactus, jumping cactus, maran, pink cedar, and frangipani.

Faunal Features

Ground doves, oystercatchers, and gray kingbirds have been seen. The crested anole and dwarf gecko are present.

Geological Features

The circumference of the island is entirely Vr showing much faulting and folding, with CrF on the higher elevations. The shoreline has several outcrops of beautiful hydrothermally altered rock in shades of red, purple, and brown.

Near Shore Features

Exposed rocks extend on the south of the island. A shallow elkhorn and sand shoal to the northeast connects the island to the mainland.

Manmade Features

None

Recommendations

Leave as unrestricted public recreation area.

Green Cay, St. Thomas

Location	18° 18' 15.45" N
	64° 54' 08" W
Owner	No record
Acres	.77 (.3 ha)
Elevation	24 ft. (7.3 m)
Shoreline	850 ft. (.26 km)

Yellow dancing lady orchid

Coconut Bay

White dancing lady orchid

Dwarf gecko
The dwarf gecko is shorter than its name in print. This small gecko, easily identified by a dark patch on its shoulders with two white spots, is usually quite abundant among dead leaves. Although it is diurnal in habit, it spends much of its time under leaves foraging for the many small insects and other invertebrates in this rich habitat. It is heavily preyed upon by larger lizards, snakes, and birds.

Boat view from the west

Opposite:
Aerial from the east

HANS LOLLICK ISLAND

One mile long, 3/4 mile wide, 1.5 miles northeast of Picara Peninsula, north shore of St. Thomas Island. So spelled on most modern charts. German, *Gross Hanslolk*; Danish, *Store Hanslolk*; Spanish, *Isla Grande de Hans-Lollik, Hansnetik*. The summit is described as *Penon Escarpado* and is marked by a triangulation station. Hansa Rock, close inshore at the south point, is 19 feet high, with an area of .11 acres. Lollik signifies a Laalander or native of *Laaland*, an island in Denmark. Thus, Hans Lollik might be either a proper name or signify, "John the Laalander"; in either case referring to some forgotten mariner or colonist.

VEGETATIONAL AND FLORAL FEATURES

This island features tyre palms in a forest on the northeast end and scattered over the island. There is a coconut palm grove, and sea grape, maho, and six species of cactus, orchids, grasses, sedges, mampo, and manchineel are present.

Hans Lollick Island

Location	18° 24' 10" N
	64° 54' 30" W
Owner	Private
Acres	489.18 (198 ha)
Elevation	704 ft. (214.5 m)
Shoreline	4.2 mi (6.75 km)

FAUNAL FEATURES

The common birds of the larger islands are found here. Donkeys and goats are present. The crested anole, barred anole, grass anole, dwarf gecko, and common ground lizard, along with the Puerto Rican racer, are present. The sand beaches provide nesting sites for hawksbill turtles. Red-billed tropicbirds nest on the rocky cliffs.

GEOLOGICAL FEATURES

Cliffs of folded igneous and sedimentary rock occur on exposed east, north, and west sides. The major soil type is CsF except for the exposed cliffs which are Vr and the sandy beach flat on the east which is JuB.

NEAR SHORE FEATURES

A fringing reef on the south and east shore provides excellent snorkeling and diving. There is a protected sandy beach on the southeast.

MANMADE FEATURES

Because of the good anchorage, boaters anchor, camp on, and litter the beach. A renovatable house, cistern and catchment, dug well, horse trough, fences, two small shacks, and a road are present. The ruins of a Dutch settlement from about 1650 are present on the south ridge.

RECOMMENDATIONS

As private land it is suitable for permanent habitation. The owners should be encouraged to plan for nondestructive use of the islands.

Boat view from the south

Tamarind fruit

Flowery century plants

Iguana

Iguanas breed from December to February and deposit their clutch of 24 to 72 eggs in a hole in March or April. After an incubation period of 2 to 3 months the brilliant green young emerge and disperse. If near houses, the young are attracted to hibiscus hedges. They become sexually mature at about age 3, with a snout vent length of about a foot. Adults eat a broad variety of wild leaves, fruits, and flowers and may damage gardens or ornamental plants. They may live to be more than 10 years of age and attain a total length of more than 6 feet while living in a typical home range of about an acre (.5 ha). The males are larger and heavier, and have more prominent dorsal spines, dewlap, and jaw shield than the females.

Opposite:
Aerial from the west

HASSEL ISLAND

Forms the western side of St. Thomas Harbor. Also known as Orkanshullet Island.

VEGETATIONAL AND FLORAL FEATURES
Most of the island is covered with dry forest. Coconut palms occur on the east and north sides while the cliffs on the west support cacti and century plants.

FAUNAL FEATURES
Most mainland birds can be seen here. The green iguana, crested anole, barred anole, common ground lizard, dwarf gecko, house gecko, Puerto Rican racer, Puerto Rican garden snake, and rats and mice are present.

GEOLOGICAL FEATURES
The many igneous, sedimentary, and metamorphic rocks including deep sea sediments now showing as rock outcrops above sea level are soil type Vr. The higher elevations are soil type CrE with intermediate elevations being CrF. There is a small sand beach on the western side and there are 3 salt ponds.

NEAR SHORE FEATURES
There are several wrecks off the southern point, and many partially exposed pilings are present off the north point. The narrow channel between St. Thomas and Hassel Island has been widened and deepened in historic times.

MANMADE FEATURES
There are many past and present modifications, including a hotel. Forts and docks have been restored, and a nonfunctional, old, steam-operated ship railway is present. Fortifications have been restored and are managed by the National Park Service.

RECOMMENDATIONS
Continue as a historical park.

Hassel Island
- **Location** 18° 20' 00" N
  64° 56' 08"
- **Owner** Private and U. S. Government
- **Acres** 139.54 (56.47 ha)
- **Elevation** 267 ft. (81.3 m)
- **Shoreline** 2.75 mi (4.42 km)

View from the south

Amygdaloidal Jasper

Lichens on boulders

Opposite: Aerial from the east

Rats
The rat commonly encountered on the small cays is the black rat (*Rattus rattus*), which is quite an attractive animal compared to the Norway rat encountered by city dwellers. The tree rat has large mobile ears and a white belly. It is nocturnal and spends much of its time in trees consuming fruits and buds. Relatively high populations may be sustained in good habitat. They compete with tree boas for den sites and seem to have an adverse effect on seabird nesting success.

HENLEY CAY

ONE OF THE THREE DURLOE CAYS

Vegetational and Floral Features
The island supports enough large trees to be called forested. These include mahogany, gumbo limbo, manchineel, and flamboyant. Sea hibiscus, frangipani, and marblewood are found on the periphery. Physic nut and inkberry are found in the interior. A large clump of bright bougainvillea planted among a cluster of huge lichen-covered boulders in 1949 is still thriving.

Faunal Features
Common ground doves, hummingbirds, gray kingbirds and Zenaida doves have been seen nesting here. Rats, the crested anole, house gecko, and dwarf gecko have been seen.

Geological Features
The island is metamorphosed volcanic rock with intrusive dikes. A sandy beach used extensively by day sailboats is on the south side. A vein of amygdaloidal jasper was mined in the past. Fragments may still be found on the beach after storms.

Near Shore Features
Rocky coral bottoms on the north, east, and west sides provide good fish habitat, but strong currents and choppy waves discourage swimming and diving.

Manmade Features
The ruins of a house are adjacent to the beach, and the foundation of a dock projects onto the beach.

Recommendations
Maintain as a multi-use recreation area.

Henley
One of the Three Durloe Cays

Location	18° 21' 20"
	64° 47' 36"
Owner	U. S. Government
Acres	11.4 (4.6 ha)
Elevation	70 ft. (21 m)
Shoreline	4100 ft. (1250 m)

Boat view from the north

Boat view from the north

Leatherback turtle
The leatherback is the largest of the sea turtles and the heaviest living reptile. They journey from the North Atlantic to the Caribbean every second year to lay 4 to 6 clutches of about 80 eggs each at 10-day intervals. They dive to depths of over 1500 feet and wander up to 50 miles offshore between nestings. The "shell" of the leatherback is flexible and covered with skin.

Opposite:
Aerial view from the west

INNER BRASS ISLAND

Island, 1,670 yards long, 853 yards wide, 3/8 mile off north shore, Little Northside Quarter, St. Thomas. Anchorage under west side, 1/2 mile offshore, Fish Point 87°. Island also called Bras, Brass, Inside Brass, *Blas Grande, Isle du Cuivre*.

VEGETATIONAL AND FLORAL FEATURES
This island is large enough and high enough to be covered by dry forest with smaller areas of croton-acacia scrub and dry forest with cactus. The vegetation has been severely altered by years of agriculture, grazing, and burning. These practices continue at the present time. Tyre palms are characteristic of the protected guts and there is a coconut grove on the southwestern corner. Century plants and cacti dominate the steep, rocky, seaside slopes.

FAUNAL FEATURES
Most of the St. Thomas bird species are found here. White-tailed tropicbirds nest here. The crested anole, barred anole, grass anole, common ground lizard, house gecko and dwarf gecko have been found. The Puerto Rican racer is very common. Rats and mice abound. Domestic animals are present. Sea turtles, including the leatherback and hawksbill, nest on the sand beaches.

GEOLOGICAL FEATURES
Except for two beaches on the western side, all shorelines are steep and rocky. A bed of red jasper can be found on the east side of the island. The largest beach is a fine white coral sand while the smaller is somewhat coarser. The highest part of the island has soil type CsE2 while the lower slopes are CsF, the steep sides are Vr, and the beaches JuB.

NEAR SHORE FEATURES
There are extensive shallows with mixed sand and coral reefs. Deeper water is present on the northern and northwestern tip.

MANMADE FEATURES
Roads, catchment area ponds, buildings, clearings, agriculture, and grazing are all a part of the landscape. At this time, it is not inhabited but has been prepared for development.

RECOMMENDATIONS
The owners should be encouraged to plan for "nondestructive" use of the islands.

Inner Brass Island
- **Location** 18° 23' 07" N 64° 58' 20" W
- **Owner** Private
- **Acres** 127.96 (51.8 ha)
- **Elevation** 256 ft. (78 m)
- **Shoreline** 2.4 mi (3.86 km)

Brown booby
Boobies are commonly seen diving with pelicans on schools of baitfish. Offshore, they catch flying fish and needlefish. They lay 2 eggs on the ground in the fall, and after a 45-day incubation period they raise only 1 chick. The chick flies at 100 days of age and then roams the Atlantic for 3 or more years before returning as an adult to breed. The same pair may nest at the same spot on an island for many years in succession. The sexes appear similar, but the females honk and the males whistle.

Leatherleaf vine

Boat view from the east

Opposite:
Aerial view from the east

Volcanic conglomerate rock formation

KALKUN CAY

Rocky, steep, narrow islet, 275 yards long, 20 to 30 yards wide, in middle of Savanna Passage, 1 mile due west of Westend of St. Thomas. Creole and Danish *Kalkun,* and Dutch *Kalkoen,* meaning "Turkey."

VEGETATIONAL AND FLORAL FEATURES

Being windsheared and mostly rock, one peak is crested with prickly pear and a plateau on the north is covered with fig. The south ridge is covered with leatherleaf.

FAUNAL FEATURES

The most notable feature is the presence of several hundred nesting brown boobies. Red-billed tropicbirds, bridled terns, roseate terns, noddy terns, and Zenaida doves also nest here. Oystercatchers are usually present on the shoreline.

GEOLOGICAL FEATURES

The entire island is composed of a complex conglomerate. A dike has eroded away, leaving a deep cleft which almost bifurcates the island.

NEAR SHORE FEATURES

The shore drops rapidly in deep water in all directions. Both sides of the island experience extremely strong reversing tidal currents.

MANMADE FEATURES

None.

RECOMMENDATIONS

Should be protected as a no-entry wildlife sanctuary.

Kalkun Cay

Location	18° 23' 54" N
	65° 04' 47" W
Owner	V. I. Government
Acres	3.53 (1.43 ha)
Elevation	73 ft. (22 m)
Shoreline	2200 ft. (0.67 km)

Boat view from the southwest showing columnar jointed rock

Opposite:
Aerial view from the north

Prickly pear cactus

Barred anole
Much smaller than crested anoles, barred anoles have a very different head profile and behavior. They commonly exhibit 3 dark blotches as dorsal saddles although these sometimes virtually disappear and a variety of reticulations take over. They are much less obvious than the crested anole and tend to keep a low profile by moving slowly and close to the substrate much in the manner of a hiding squirrel. A female was observed digging a nest cavity in moist clay soil. She did this by using the front feet and depositing the material behind her between the hind legs. At the completion of the excavation, she turned and deposited 2 soft white eggs into the 2-inch-deep burrow. She then took each egg, in turn, in her mouth and carefully rubbed it on the chamber walls until it was entirely clay-colored. Then she covered the eggs by pushing and tamping dirt with her muzzle in the way that a dog buries a bone.

LEDUCK ISLAND

Islet, 100 yards wide, 600 yards long, lying 1/2 mile southeast of Sabbat Point and midway between Moor Point and Ram Head at Coral Bay entrance, St. John. Gerard van Keulen (1719) named it *Peter Le Duck's Eyland*, presumably for a Flemish Colonist. Later called Duck's Island, Duck Island, Duck Cay, Buck Island, *Boken Eyland, Islita Borgem, Isla Duck o Buck o Borgem*, etc. Present name adopted November 7, 1923, to distinguish this from three other cays in Virgin Islands known as Buck I, Summit, and Coral Knoll.

VEGETATIONAL AND FLORAL FEATURES
The cliffs of Leduck are dominated by Turkscap cactus, while sea grapes are dense on the south side. Prickly pear cactus with large edible fruit occur on top of the eastern ridge. Black mangroves occupy the salt pond on the north of the island.

FAUNAL FEATURES
Ground lizards, crested anoles, barred anoles, house geckos, dwarf geckos, and slipperyback skinks are present. Zenaida doves nest in the black mangroves.

GEOLOGICAL FEATURES
Leduck is composed of intrusive volcanic rock cut by many dikes. The shoreline is steep, with many notches. There is a single salt pond behind the rubble beach on the north side. The higher elevations are CrF with Vr on the periphery except the JuB beach.

NEAR SHORE FEATURES
There are coral formations on all sides with a shallow elkhorn reef to the north. The northwest bay is usually a protected anchorage allowing interesting snorkeling.

MANMADE FEATURES
None.

RECOMMENDATIONS
Leave unmodified as a wildlife sanctuary.

Leduck Island	
Location	18° 19' 08" N
	64° 41' 20" W
Owner	V.I. Government
Acres	13.518 (5.69 ha)
Elevation	85 ft. (25.9 m)
Shoreline	1.0 mi (1.6 km)

Boat view from the east

Laughing gull flying

Hawksbill turtle
The attractive markings of the shell of the hawksbill result in demand for it in the fabrication of jewelry and trinkets. The population, endangered by excessive harvest (including eggs), is now fully protected and appears to be locally recovering. Hawskbills may regularly be seen resting or feeding on invertebrates and sponges in coral reef areas. They nest among the vegetation on the landward side of most beaches in the Virgin Islands and, unlike other sea turtles, do not require a sandy beach.

Opposite: Aerial view from the south

LITTLE HANS LOLLICK ISLAND

Island, 1,000 yards long, 700 yards wide, lying 310 yards north of Hans-Lollik, to which it is joined by a coral ledge; 2 1/2 miles northeast of Picara Point and 3 1/4 miles west-southwest of Little Tobago. Other names are translations: Danish, *Lille Hanslollik*; Spanish, *Isla Chica de Hans-Lollik*; German, *Klein Hanslolk*.

VEGETATIONAL AND FLORAL FEATURES
The vegetation is low and wind-sheared on the east side of the island. The west side is covered with closed canopy vegetation. There is a coconut grove on the south side behind the beach.

FAUNAL FEATURES
Zenaida doves and laughing gulls nest here. Many of the St. Thomas birds are found here on occasion. The barred anole, grass anole, dwarf gecko, common ground lizard, and Puerto Rican racer have all been seen. European rabbits were introduced in 1972, and hawksbill turtles nest on the beach.

GEOLOGICAL FEATURES
The island shows large-scale folding of conglomerate layers cut by dikes. The exposed cliffs are Vr with the higher elevations CsE2 and CsF. The spectacular beach on the southeast is JuB.

NEAR SHORE FEATURES
A shallow elkhorn coral reef to the southeast provides excellent snorkeling.

MANMADE FEATURES
None.

RECOMMENDATIONS
Utilize as a multipurpose recreation area under either private or government operation.

Little Hans Lollick Island

Location	18° 24' 40" N
	64° 54' 30" W
Owner	Private
Acres	100.48 (40.66 ha)
Elevation	204 ft. (62.17 m)
Shoreline	2 mi (3.2 km)

Boat view from
the southwest

Opposite:
Aerial view from
the east

Manchineel tree

White-tail deer

Deer were first introduced to the Virgin Islands from the eastern U. S. in 1792, with subsequent introductions from Texas and Georgia. They have adapted very well to the ecological circumstances in the Virgin Islands and seem to do well in all habitats from the wettest to the dryest. Does weigh about 80 pounds, and bucks average about 100. Births occur in almost any month. Bucks usually shed their antlers in late fall and begin regrowth shortly thereafter. If undisturbed, deer live very well in the presence of humans, as evidenced by the resident deer populations at Estate Cotton Valley on St. Croix and Estate Nazareth on St. Thomas.

LITTLE ST. JAMES ISLAND

Island, 1,000 yards long, south-southeast of Great St. James Island. Variant forms of name: *Klyn St. Jems, Petit St.James, Lille James Eyland, Santiago Chico*.

VEGETATIONAL AND FLORAL FEATURES
The woolly nipple cactus is common while most of the island is covered with dry forest and wind-sheared shrub. A manchineel grove is present behind the western beach.

FAUNAL FEATURES
The common ground lizard, barred anole, crested anole, grass anole, house gecko, dwarf gecko, and Puerto Rican racer are present. Doves and tropicbirds nest on the south side. The many rats present may have contributed to the 100% nest loss of the roseate terns nesting there in 1977.

GEOLOGICAL FEATURES
The island is layered metamorphic and igneous rocks cut by many dikes. Two salt ponds are present. The highest elevations are CrE surrounded by CrF with the periphery composed of Vr and four JuB beaches.

NEAR SHORE FEATURES
A shallow grass bed with many queen conchs is present to the west. The southwest cove is used frequently by commercial scuba tours.

MANMADE FEATURES
A pier on the west side and a multi-structured private residence on the north ridge were built in 1987.

RECOMMENDATIONS
Multipurpose residential and nature preserve.

Little St. James Island
Location	18° 18' 06" N
	64° 49' 37" W
Owner	Private
Acres	68.73 (27.8 ha)
Elevation	142 ft. (43.3 m)
Shoreline	2.2 mi (3.54 km)

Boat view from the north

Pinguin (bromeliad)

Mongoose
The small Indian mongoose was introduced to the Caribbean in 1872 to control rats in sugarcane fields. It does not swim well, but it has been widely introduced by humans. It is a small but ferocious predator which has devastated many island species unaccustomed to terrestrial carnivores. It is diurnal and can be seen by day on St. Croix, St. Thomas, and St. John.

Opposite:
Aerial from the southeast

LOVANGO CAY

Island, 1,800 yards long, 300 yards wide, 1 mile northwest of Hognest Point, St. John, separated from Mingo Cay on west by shoal passage 300 yards wide.

VEGETATIONAL AND FLORAL FEATURES
Dry forest interspersed with maran and *Acacia* scrub covers the island irregularly. The vegetation has been highly modified by agriculture and grazing. The spiney bromeliad, locally called pinguin, was used as a living livestock fence and now grows randomly throughout the island.

FAUNAL FEATURES
Lovango Cay is a popular location for seabird roosting. Wilson's plovers, common ground doves, and smooth-billed anis nest here. The common ground lizard, crested anole, grass anole, house gecko, and Puerto Rican racer are present. Mongooses were introduced on the cay, however, it is believed that they have all been subsequently killed.

GEOLOGICAL FEATURES
Steep cliffs of various metamorphic rock with strata tilted almost vertically mark much of the north side. Large garnets are abundant in the rock on the west end. The higher elevations are CsF while the shorelines are Vr except for a long JuB sandy beach on the south and a shorter one on the north.

NEAR SHORE FEATURES
Off the JuB beach to the north a shallow reef is available and popular for snorkeling. A turtle grass bed is found off the southwest beach.

MANMADE FEATURES
The island has long been inhabited (pop. 20) and, at the time of purchase by the U. S. in 1917, a public school existed on Lovango. Today there are several small houses on the south side of the island. There are two piers and the pilings of a third on this same shoreline.

RECOMMENDATIONS
Continue the present use for low-density single family dwellings.

Lovango Cay
- **Location** 18° 21' 50" N
  64° 48' 30" W
- **Owner** Private
- **Acres** 117.979 (47.74 ha)
- **Elevation** 255 ft. (77 m)
- **Shoreline** 2.6 mi (4.18 km)

Aerial view from the east

Red-billed tropicbird nest

Folded marble with silicate nodule

Boat view from the south

Wooly nipple cactus

Opposite: Aerial from the west

Ground lizard
An active and aggressive terrestrial predator, the ground lizard feeds on anything it can overpower, including crabs and other lizards. It will also scavenge a broad variety of items, including crumbs from a picnic. The young animals are striped, but the more mature animals are speckled. It is most active in the hot part of the day. It exhibits the short, rapid, jerky movements which are characteristic of the family and anthropomorphically are very "nervous" animals.

MINGO CAY

Island, 1,170 yards long, 258 yards wide, middle link in chain with Grass Cay on west and Lovango Cay on east. Spanish alternative name, *Lovango Medio*; also called *Senior, Sinjo, Singo*.

VEGETATIONAL AND FLORAL FEATURES
The island is covered with a dry forest, including Jamaica caper and three patches of maran and *Acacia* scrub. The south shoreline has many clumps of woolly nipple and turkscap cactus on the rocks.

Mingo Cay
Location	18° 21' 42" N
	69° 49' 15" W
Owner	Private
Acres	48.35 (19.56 ha)
Elevation	186 ft. (56.7 m)
Shoreline	1.4 mi (2.25 km)

FAUNAL FEATURES
Red-billed tropicbirds nest in the rocks. Also present are the common ground lizard, crested anole, dwarf gecko, and Puerto Rican racer. Goats are present.

GEOLOGICAL FEATURES
Both igneous and metamorphic rocks are present on the island. The north side of the cay is marked by steep, rocky cliffs (Vr), while soil type CsF slopes to the shore on the south. Perhaps of greatest interest is the marble outcrop on the southeast side, with several deep caves produced by ground water solution. A JuB beach is on the southwest corner.

NEAR SHORE FEATURES
A reef fringes the southwest portion of the cay, and on the north deep water comes to the base of the cliffs. A wreck lies in 60 ft. of water off the southwest tip.

MANMADE FEATURES
None

RECOMMENDATIONS
Encourage the removal of livestock and use-sensitive environmental management..

Jamaican fruit-eating bat

Mampo tree

Opposite:
Aerial view
from the east

Boat view
from the east

Cave bat
The cave bat is found by day in dark roosts in rock crevices, caves, or ruins. Bats in roosts composed exclusively of females who give birth synchronously in the spring. For the first several weeks they carry their young while foraging. They prefer to feed on nectar and pollen when trees such as the West Indian locust are blooming. They also consume the fleshy fruits of many other trees such as manjack. These bats are very fractious, and the roosts may often be located by the sounds of loud bickering among the occupants.

OUTER BRASS ISLAND

Island, 1,400 yards long, 720 yards wide, 1 1/2 miles off north coast of St. Thomas. Also called Outside Bras or Brass, and *Rondomlelyk*.

VEGETATIONAL AND FLORAL FEATURES
Covered with dry forest on the higher portions. The windward side of the northern peninsula has areas of sedge and grass probably initiated by burning but now maintained by wind shear.

FAUNAL FEATURES
Most St. Thomas bird species are found here. Red-billed and white-tailed tropicbirds nest on the cliffs. Large groups of brown boobies and laughing gulls rest on and fish from the rocks at Rough Out Point on the north. The crested anole, barred anole, common ground lizard, dwarf gecko, and Puerto Rican racer are common. Rats and mice have found their way to the cay. Domestic animals have been introduced. Fishing and Jamaican fruit-eating bats use the sea cave on the north end.

GEOLOGICAL FEATURES
The steep rocky limestone cliffs are stratified, dramatically tilted, and intermingled with other metamorphic and igneous rocks. Near Rough Out Point these tilted slabs form the roof of a large sea cave which can be entered by a small boat on calm days. The high southern peak has soil type CsF bordered to the north by Ls and still further north by CsF. Another cave is on the southwest corner.

NEAR SHORE FEATURES
Though this cay is surrounded by deeper waters than many others, there is nevertheless a shoal at the southeast end and a dramatic submerged rock just west of Rough Out Point.

MANMADE FEATURES
Because of the difficulty of access the cay has not been as heavily utilized as Inner Brass, but domestic animals have long been grazed there.

RECOMMENDATIONS
Should remain as a wildlife management area. The difficulty of landing safely precludes regular recreational use, but "bird watching" from a boat can be a unique experience. The goats should be removed.

Outer Brass Island
Location	18° 24' 00" N
	64° 58' 17" W
Owner	V. I. Government
Acres	107.95 (43.69 ha)
Elevation	412 ft. (725.5 m)
Shoreline	2.2 mi (3.54 km)

Red mangrove fruit

Boat view from the south

Black-necked stilt

Opposite:
Aerial view
from the north

Territoriality in the barred anole

Over a period of several weeks, 2 males were observed in territorial encounters that often lasted several hours. They had established themselves on the patio of a house. While they utilized the ornate block wall and furniture as part of their foraging and basking territory, only the tile floor was used in their encounters, which were very different from those of the crested anole. At the beginning of an encounter, erectile tissue produced both nuchal and vertebral dorsal "sails." The three body blotches faded and a fine lenticular body pattern appeared on a pale translucent greenish-grey background. About an inch of the tail tip became nearly black, and the area around the eyes and across the top of the head became tinted with blue. While remaining about a foot apart, they warily circled broadside to one another. Simultaneously, the gular fans were rhythmically and slowly extended and the heads were deliberately raised and lowered. Suddenly, the feet were bunched as if to leap, the gular fans were extended and short rapid pumping motions of the body were made, with the necks bowed and snouts turned upward. At the same time, the tongues were fully extended and engorged as bright red "flags." This was followed by each animal sprawling spread-eagled on the tile with one side of the head pressed down tightly and one eye uppermost so that they looked as if someone had stepped on them. Finally, they sometimes locked jaws as the crested anole does.

PATRICIA CAY

One-half mile long, chiefly a mangrove swamp immediately south of Bovoni Cay, and terminating in a 75-foot knoll or humpel at Patrick Point, St. Thomas.

VEGETATIONAL AND FLORAL FEATURES
Red mangrove is the dominant vegetation. On the highest point at the eastern end is dry forest with cactus.

FAUNAL FEATURES
Patricia Cay was formerly a nesting area for wading birds. Deer are sometimes present. Rats are common. The crested anole, barred anole, green iguana, house gecko, dwarf gecko, and Puerto Rican racer are present.

Patricia Cay
- **Location** 18° 14' 00" N
  64° 52' 20" W
- **Owner** Private
- **Acres** 33.4 (13.5 ha)
- **Elevation** 75 ft. (22.8 m)
- **Shoreline** 1.3 mi (2.09 km)

GEOLOGICAL FEATURES
Sometimes considered a portion of Bovoni Cay, it features a large inner pond. Patricia Point on the southern tip is a very steep cliff of metamorphic rock with quartz veins with CsF on top. The southern side is JuB beach, and the remainder is T5 mangroves.

NEAR SHORE FEATURES
An interesting reef and shoal connect to Cas Cay and extend from the south to a well-developed spur and groove formation offshore.

MANMADE FEATURES
In the 1960s a canal was dredged between the west side and St. Thomas.

RECOMMENDATIONS
Should be purchased as a wildlife preserve and made part of the territorial park system.

Jasper in conglomerate

Sea Purslane
This prostrate plant seldom reaches a foot in height but may form dense carpets of growth on the sand above the high-water line. Depending on growing conditions, the normally dark green leaves may be bright cherry red. The thick, fleshy leaves are crisp and tender; although somewhat salty, they make an interesting addition to a salad. Some populations of the plant have white flowers rather than the usual pink.

Boat view from the east

Sandwich tern

Opposite: Aerial view from the southwest

PELICAN CAY

Cay, 220 yards long, 110 yards off north shore of Little Hans Lollik Island. Frequented by pelicans, hence name. *Kropgie* a local synonym. *Nordoe*, Danish *Nordø* means North Island. Not to be confused with other Pelican Island, 2 miles east of St. John. This cay had no official name till christened by the Coast Geodetic Survey, but was described in Spanish as *Isolotillo, bajo y Penascoso* (an islet, low and rocky having at the north a reef—*Escollo*).

VEGETATIONAL AND FLORAL FEATURES
Several small patches of buttonwood and leatherleaf, jumping cactus, turkscap cactus, and beach pea along with scattered patches of sea purslane and portulaca all nestle in rock crevices for protection from strong wind and spray.

Pelican Cay
Location	18° 21' 00" N
	64° 54' 32" W
Owner	Private
Acres	4.5 (1.82 ha)
Elevation	30 ft. (9.1 m)
Shoreline	225 yds. (.2 km)

FAUNAL FEATURES
The roseate tern nests here regularly, and sandwich terns nested in 1978 and 1987. Laughing gulls and oystercatchers nest sporadically.

GEOLOGICAL FEATURES
Pelican Cay is the most northerly of the American Virgins and is composed of metamorphic conglomerate. Chunks of vivid red jasper are present in the central area of the cay.

NEAR SHORE FEATURES
Deep water with lush coral growth exists on all sides except on the south which connects to Little Hans Lollick by a shoal.

MANMADE FEATURES
None

RECOMMENDATIONS
Not suitable for human habitation. Encourage the owner to maintain as a "no-entry" wildlife area.

Roseate tern flying

Windswept vegetation

Terrestrial hermit crab

The terrestrial hermit crab has a soft body which it protects by backing into a snail shell. The shell aids in water conservation and may even carry a store of water. In late August, legions of crabs in narrow trails may be seen descending from the mountains to the sea. Huge aggregations occur at certain traditional places on the shoreline as the crabs prepare to spawn in their annual visit to the sea. After laying 1,000 to 50,000 eggs they return to the uplands. As the crabs grow, they abandon the old shell and move into a larger shell. They eat a great variety of plant and animal matter but seem to have a particular preference for ripe fruit and may climb into trees to forage.

Opposite: Aerial view from the southwest

Boat view from the southeast

PERKINS CAY

Islet, 60 yards in diameter, west of Denis Bay, east of Hognest Bay entrance northwestern shore of St. John.

VEGETATIONAL AND FLORAL FEATURES
Low wind-sheared scrub of sea grape on the highest level with leatherleaf, inkberry, and sedges in soil pockets.

FAUNAL FEATURES
Visited by birds from the very near shore of St. John.

GEOLOGICAL FEATURES
An interesting shoal and reef connect Perkins Cay and St. John.

MANMADE FEATURES
None

RECOMMENDATIONS
Acquisition by the National Park Service.

Perkins Cay
Location 18° 21' 23" N
64° 46' 38" W
Owner V. I. Government
Acres .56 (.22 ha)
Elevation 25 ft. (7.6 m)
Shoreline 262 yds. (.239 km)

Snowy egret

Coconut palm

Boat view from the east

St. Croix anole
About the same size as the crested anole, it lives without competition from other anole species and is thus able to expand its range, habitat, and habits into those niches normally occupied by another species. In contrast to those species in the northern islands, it is often extremely wary and does not allow close human approach, while the crested anole will often jump onto a human body and even feed from one's fingers.

Mahogany tree with fruit

Opposite: Aerial view from the west

PROTESTANT CAY

Islet, 300 yards long. Flagstaff marked pilot station (Danish, *Lods*); whence sometimes called *Lodskalen*. The Catholic French in possession of St. Croix 1650-1696 buried Protestant Huguenots on this island, giving it the name Protestant Cay. Called by Spanish *Cayo Protestante*; by Dutch, *Loots* (= pilots) *Kay*; by Danish, *Protestantkai*; by Ledru, *Illot au nord de la Ville*.

VEGETATIONAL AND FLORAL FEATURES

Coconut palms have been planted on the southern part of the island. Exotic plants have been planted around the hotel and in the small manmade ponds on the south side. Some large tamarind and mahogany trees still remain around the hotel, while mangrove trees are still present on the east shore. Tan tan trees and cacti are also present on the east side.

FAUNAL FEATURES

Many St. Croix birds visit the island. The St. Croix anole and dwarf gecko are present. The endangered St. Croix ground lizard is found only here and on Green Cay to the east. Tilapia were introduced into the small manmade ponds.

GEOLOGICAL FEATURES

The island, which narrows to a point on the north, has sandy beaches on the south and west sides. Soil types are JuB on the west and south with the remainder being DeD. The sandy beach provides potential turtle nesting sites.

NEAR SHORE FEATURES

The cay is situated in the harbor of Christiansted, St. Croix. Reefs present at the mouth of the harbor to the northwest protect the north and west part of the island. Due to the reef, there is shallow water immediately to the northwest. However, the water is open and deep on the south and east. The mainland is about 300 yards away.

MANMADE FEATURES

Protestant Cay is the former site of Fort Sofia Frederika. A hotel now dominates the center of the island. A house is located on the north point. Concrete breakwaters are on the western and southern beaches, and a concrete pier extends 20 feet into the water on the south shore. Manmade ponds are present, as are a swimming pool, tennis court, shuffleboard, and a wooden pier on the east side.

RECOMMENDATIONS

The human inhabitants of this tiny cay should be made aware of the endangered status and limited habitat of *Ameiva polops* and thus initiate specific programs and activities aimed at preserving the population.

Protestant Cay

Location	17° 57' 16" N
	64° 42' 03" W
Owner	V. I. Government
Acres	7.1 (2.87 ha)
Elevation	33 ft. (10 m)
Shoreline	525 yds. (.48 km)

Boat view from the south

Portulaca flower

Cobble in conglomerate

Opposite: Aerial view from the west

Wind-sheared manchineel tree

RAMGOAT CAY

ONE OF THE THREE DURLOE CAYS

One hundred eighty yards long, second in size of Durloe Cays, 310 yards east-northeast of Henley Cay, 330 yards northwest of Hognest Peninsula, northwest shore of St. John Island. "Ramgoat" is a kind of bush, *Fagara tragodes*

VEGETATIONAL AND FLORAL FEATURES
Turkscap, dildo, and jumping cactus are common throughout with inkberry, gumbo limbo, and frangipani at the higher elevations. Sea grape, portulaca, and limber caper grow at the edge of the shoreline cliffs.

FAUNAL FEATURES
Common ground doves and Zenaida doves nest here, and the crested anole has been collected.

GEOLOGICAL FEATURES
The island is primarily metamorphic conglomerate rock that includes chunks of fossil-bearing limestone. A lava flow is exposed on the northeast side.

NEAR SHORE FEATURES
Deep water exposed to large waves and a strong current is present on the east, north, and west sides. The south side is more protected and allows snorkeling and landing on the shoreline of polished rocks.

MANMADE FEATURES
None

RECOMMENDATIONS
Maintain in present undeveloped state.

Ramgoat
One of the three Durloe Cays

Location	18° 21' 26" N
	64° 47' 24" W
Owner	U. S. Government
Acres	2.7 (1.0 ha)
Elevation	30 ft. (9 m)
Shoreline	1203 ft. (.367 km)

Boat view from the east

Immature yellow-crowned night heron

Opposite: Aerial view from the east

Woolly nipple cactus on cliff face

Crested anole

The crested anole is the most common lizard in the northern Virgin Islands. It perches and forages on insects on the lower trunks of trees and the adjacent ground. Hard-shelled, white, almost spherical eggs are deposited in protected crevices. The males develop a conspicuous dorsal crest from the base of the skull to the tail. This crest may be further erected and the dewlap extended when in a territorial dispute with another male.

RATA CAY

ONE OF THE THREE DURLOE CAYS

Eighty yards long, smallest of Durloe Cays, 400 yards northwest of Henley Cay, 770 yards southeast of Lovango Cay, off northwest shore of St. John Island. Spanish, *Rata*, "Rat."

VEGETATIONAL AND FLORAL FEATURES
The expected seaside plants such as sea purslane, portulaca, and beach pea, along with turkscap, *mammillaria*, and dildo cactus are present. A tangle of limber caper, leather leaf, and fig crown the upper parts of the island which receive less spray.

FAUNAL FEATURES
The crested anole along with oystercatchers and yellow-crowned night herons are regular inhabitants. Laughing gulls nest here in the spring.

GEOLOGICAL FEATURES
The island is composed of highly weathered volcanic and conglomerate rock.

NEAR SHORE FEATURES
The wave wash zone is rocky with many urchins and fire coral. Strong reversing tidal currents make diving difficult on the fringing coral areas.

MANMADE FEATURES
None.

RECOMMENDATIONS
Maintain in present undeveloped state.

Rata
One of the three Durloe Cays

Location	18° 21' 29" N
	64° 47' 50" W
Owner	U. S. Government
Acres	.51 (.2 ha)
Elevation	15 ft. (4.6 m)
Shoreline	900 ft. (.274 km)

Soldier Crab in West Indian top shell

Jumping cactus

Boat view from the east

White mangrove fruit

Manchineel
This small tree commonly grows near the sea and bears greenish-yellow apple-like fruit about 1 inch in diameter. The sap is highly irritating to the skin and eyes. Even light contact with the leaves or bark can produce a reaction. Smoke from burning leaves or wood is also damaging to eyes and lungs. Symptoms of vomiting, pain, and digestive tract bleeding may be delayed up to 2 hours after eating the sweet, aromatic, delicious fruit. Deaths have occurred.

Opposite: Aerial view from the south

ROTTO CAY

Islet, 150 yards long, 170 yards south of Compass Point, in Jersey Bay, Redhook Quarter, St. Thomas. Called by the Dutch, *Roode Eyland*; by the French, *Isle Rouge*.

VEGETATIONAL AND FLORAL FEATURES
Fifteen species of woody plants, including red, white, and black mangrove, gumbo limbo, and manchineel, are present on the low-lying north corner of the cay. Cacti, including prickly pear, dildo, and turkscap, along with bromeliads, guinea grass, limber caper, maran, and frangipani are present.

Rotto Cay
Location	18° 18' 58" N
	64° 51' 53" W
Owner	Private
Acres	2.0 (.8 ha)
Elevation	33 ft. (10 m)
Shoreline	1200 ft. (.36 km)

FAUNAL FEATURES
The shoals are fishing grounds for herons, egrets, and brown pelicans, while many other species of birds visit from nearby St. Thomas. Deer have been observed here, as have the crested anole, dwarf gecko, and common ground lizard.

GEOLOGICAL FEATURES
The eastern portion of the island is marked by a sheer cliff face of lava cut by quartz dikes with some crystals over an inch in diameter. There is a JuB beach on the northwest corner and CrE on the higher parts of the cay.

NEAR SHORE FEATURES
Interesting reefs and shoals exist along the shore. There is a sand bar from the northern tip nearly to the manglar lying to the northwest.

MANMADE FEATURES
A harbor entrance marker has been painted on the rock of the southeast corner.

RECOMMENDATIONS
Acquire as part of the territorial park system and a protective buffer zone for Benner Bay.

Opposite: Aerial view from the east

Boat view from the northeast

Nicker bean

Audubon's shearwater
This attractive little bird may be seen at sea flying with a rapid flutter and short glides. In calm weather it may be seen in flocks pattering and running across the surface of the ocean as it catches small floating and surface-dwelling organisms. In the Virgin Islands it lays a single white egg in small caves or holes in winter, spring, and summer. The downy young are a dusky gray in color and are usually left alone in the burrow as the parents forage at sea during the day. The call is an eerie ululating howl given almost solely at night. If you are anchored in a quiet cove and hear a ghost it is almost surely a shearwater.

Sooty tern

SABA ISLAND

Triangular island, 575 yards long, 2 3/8 miles southwest of Red Point, 22 miles west of Flamingo Point, and 1 mile beyond Flat Cays. There being another Saba Island in the West Indies, 110 miles east-southeast of St. Thomas. Saba Cay is better known as Little Saba; Danish, *Lille Saba*; Dutch, *Klyn Sabbath*; German, *Klein Saba oder Sabbath*; French, *Petit Isle de Saba, Isle du Sabbat*, or *Isle à Crabe*. The Spanish retain one of its earliest names, *Montalvan*.

VEGETATIONAL AND FLORAL FEATURES

The exposed ridges are covered with guinea grass, mixed on the central ridge with turkscap cactus and on the west ridge with tan-tan. On the leeward side of the east ridge is a dry forest slope. The northern coral rubble berm is colonized by button mangrove and nickers. Behind the sandy beach to the west is a dense stand of manchineel. The salt ponds are surrounded by black mangrove.

FAUNAL FEATURES

The crested anole, barred anole, house gecko, dwarf gecko, and slipperyback skink along with the Puerto Rican racer are present. In order of abundance the nesting seabirds are sooty terns (over 5000 pairs), laughing gulls, roseate terns, noddy terns, and Audubon's shearwater. Terrestrial nesting birds include Zenaida doves, common ground doves, white-cheeked pintail duck, Antillean crested hummingbird, and bananaquit. A sooty tern banded on 8 July 1963 in the dry Tortugas of Florida was found nesting on Saba 21 July 1979. This was the first record of this species nesting at other than its hatching location. Hawksbill turtles nest on the beaches.

GEOLOGICAL FEATURES

Two salt ponds are present behind the northern rubble beach. The southern and western shores are precipitous Vr. The steep north-facing slopes are CrF and the lower slopes are CrE. There is a small JuB sand beach on the northwest corner. Contrary to local folklore, there is no evidence of a recent volcanic eruption.

NEAR SHORE FEATURES

A shallow sandbar reaches north to Turtledove Cay and a shallow reef lies to the northeast off the rubble beach. A grass bed is under the shallow western waters and is bordered by an emergent rock on the north.

MANMADE FEATURES

The island has been used as a military target, and fragments of ordnance remain. A fiberglass water catchment (game guzzler) has been installed. The area has been used to raise domestic stock (especially fighting cocks), and the sea bird colonies have been traditionally egged.

RECOMMENDATION

The island's status as a game reserve under Virgin Islands law should be maintained.

Saba Island
- *Location* 18° 18' 18" N
  65° 00' 00" W
- *Owner* V. I. Government
- *Acres* 30.296 (12.26 ha)
- *Elevation* 202 ft. (61.56 m)
- *Shoreline* 1.0 mi (1.6 km)

Female magnificent frigatebird

Boat view from the northeast

Opposite: Aerial view from the south

Turkscap cactus
An atypical "barrel cactus" with a prominent red cap (*cephalium*) somewhat resembling the hats favored by the Turks, which accounts for its name. With a range from the southern Bahamas to Dominica, it is common on rocky ground sometimes in salt spray. It even grows from cracks on vertical cliffs. The conical pink fruit is edible and is consumed by many island animals from birds to anole lizards.

SAIL ROCK

Remarkable, round, steep rugged, barren, double-pointed, whitish-gray islet, 100 yards in diameter, situated in Virgin Passage, 3 1/4 miles southwest of Savana Island and 6 miles southwest of west end of St. Thomas. Resembles a vessel under sail whence all the many names applied to it: *Bergantin Carabela*, Caravel, Caravella, Carvel of St. Thomas, *Caravalla, Franske Seiler, Galliot, Karavelle, La Caravelle, La Galiote, La Roca Caravela, Le Heu, Hoy, Galiota Fransmanuar* (French man-of-war), *Roca Carvel*, etc. Oldendorp's *Missions-Geshichte* contains this excellent description: "Steep rock, with two peaks, which is entirely white from the guano of the birds, has this name, because at a distance it has a resemblance to this kind of Spanish vessel." During the American Revolution, the story goes, the captain of a French frigate was so deceived by the appearance of Sail Rock that he actually hailed it. The echo created the illusion of a return fire, and a hot cannonade was continued throughout the night. In 1922, a cargo boat of lighthouse tender Lilac circled inaccessible cliffs and discovered on the west side a little bay sheltered from easterly trade winds and a marine cave, 25 by 100 feet, terraced at rear with an opening through roof 45 feet to the top of a jagged shelf, above which is an 80-foot vertical crag.

VEGETATIONAL AND FLORAL FEATURES
A bright green moss grows under a rocky overhang on the south side and in the transverse cave. A small number of turkscap cactus have colonized the northern slope.

FAUNAL FEATURES
The roseate tern, bridled tern, noddy tern, red-billed tropicbird, and brown booby are regularly present and probably nest. Magnificent frigatebirds regularly roost on the higher elevations.

GEOLOGICAL FEATURES
Guano, which colors the island white, is present except at the waterline, which is higher on the windward side.

MANMADE FEATURES
The foundation and remains of a navigation light are at the peak of the island. Further down on the north side is a concrete battery storage building which was serviced by a crane whose concrete foundation is still present on the northern cliff.

RECOMMENDATIONS
Retain as a seabird sanctuary.

Sail Rock
Location 18° 17' 00" N
65° 06' 00" W
Owner V. I. Government
Acres 1.6 (.65 ha)
Elevation 125 ft. (38.1 m)
Shoreline 1000 ft. (.3 km)

Slipperyback skink

Boat view from the south

Opposite: Aerial view from the west

Roof bat
The roof bat commonly roosts beneath galvanized roofs in spaces where the air temperature may exceed 125° F. These are the first bats to be seen in the evening, as they often begin to capture insects before dusk. Their agile flight with frequent abrupt changes of direction make them easy to identify in the Virgin Islands. At less than .5 ounce in weight, they are the smallest bat in the Virgin Islands, but each individual may eat several hundred mosquitoes per night.

SALT CAY

Island, .5 mile long, northwest of West Cay, 7/8 mile from west end of St. Thomas. Salt Key on some maps.

VEGETATIONAL AND FLORAL FEATURES
The south-facing slopes of the northern ridge are covered with guinea grass, while the lower areas surrounding the salt pond are covered with dry forest.

FAUNAL FEATURES
The common ground lizard, crested anole, dwarf gecko, and slipperyback skink are present. Zenaida dove nests have been found here, and many other bird species from St. Thomas probably nest here. Roof bats are commonly seen feeding on flying insects near the island. The island was routinely used to pasture livestock.

GEOLOGICAL FEATURES
The cliffs (especially precipitous on the north) are Vr. The highest crowns are CsF while the lower elevations are CsF2. The rock on the island is a highly variable conglomerate with vertical dikes. The JuB beach and berm on the east separate the salt pond from the sea.

NEAR SHORE FEATURES
A shallow bar separates Salt Cay from the western tip of West Cay. Strong reversing tidal rips flow to the south, west, and north of the cay.

MANMADE FEATURES
None.

RECOMMENDATIONS
Utilize as multipurpose wildlife refuge and recreation area.

Salt Cay
Location	18° 21' 46" N
	64° 03' 17" W
Owner	V. I. Government
Acres	55.81 (22.5 ha)
Elevation	242 ft. (73.75 m)
Shoreline	1.75 mi (2.8 km)

Eastern shoreline view from the east

Christmas orchid

Cliff face boat view from the west

St. Thomas worm lizard
This legless lizard looks much like an earthworm in size, color, annular body rings, and lack of visible eyes. It is quite common (except in very dry weather) in forested areas where there is leaf litter and loose surface rocks. It probably feeds on anything it can catch as it moves readily backward and forward in its burrow like an earthworm does. There are many other species of "worm lizards" in the world, and only one of these is known to produce living young. Many lay their eggs in ant and termite nests. It is not known where it deposits its eggs.

Opposite: Aerial view from the south

Blind snake
This tan to pink burrowing snake is blind and, in contrast to the worm lizard, is highly polished like a smooth wax candle, usually smaller than a soda straw. It feeds on termites and ants. Among the 200 or so related species, some lay eggs and some bear living young. We are not certain about the reproductive habits of this blind snake. Members of the genus have a small spine at the tip of the short, stubby tail. They press this spine into the skin of a person handling them and, although it is perfectly harmless, many people consider them to have a deadly sting. It seems to be much less common than the worm lizard in similar habitat in the Virgin Islands.

SAVANA ISLAND

One mile long, .5 mile wide, 2 miles west-southwest of Westend Point of St. Thomas. Island used as goat farm (Spanish *cabral*); overgrown with "catch-and-keep" vines (*Acacia ripara*), small trees, and underbrush. Name variously spelled by early cartographers: Savaan, Savane, Savannah, Savanna; also called *Cabrita* or *Cabrito* and Green Island; erroneously, *Klein St. Thomas*. A rocky reef extends 300 yards eastward, described as *una Cadena de Rocas limpias, acantiladas* (a chain of rocks clear, steep).

VEGETATIONAL AND FLORAL FEATURES
The west side is covered with groves of tyre palm and frangipani. Prostrate sea grape, grasses, and sedges are present at the waterline. On the south and east are windswept matted vegetation clumps composed of acacias and maran.

Savana Island
Location	18° 20' 30" N
	64° 04' 50" W
Owner	V. I. Government
Acres	173.862 (70.3 ha)
Elevation	269 ft. (90 m)
Shoreline	3.1 mi (5 km)

FAUNAL FEATURES
The Puerto Rican racer, common ground lizard, crested anole, barred anole, dwarf gecko, and St. Thomas worm lizard are recorded. Most of the bird species from St. Thomas and Culebra visit the island. White-crowned and scaly-naped pigeons nest here. Goats are present.

GEOLOGICAL FEATURES
The north and west shorelines are marked by steep Vr conglomerate cliffs with caves and jumbled boulders which have fallen into the sea. The south and east have exposed and tilted/sedimentary Vr strata. There is a shallow cave on the north side. The interior of the island is CsF2 surrounded by steeper CsF soil.

NEAR SHORE FEATURES
There is varied reef development on the east side, and a shallow ridge trends to the east-northeast with a group of emergent rocks. There is a large deep protected cove on the west side which provides scenic scuba diving.

MANMADE FEATURES
It was once used as a goat farm. On the southwest peak a helicopter landing area provides service for a navigation light at 300 ft.

RECOMMENDATIONS
Remove the goats and utilize as a multipurpose wildlife refuge and recreation area. The size and features of the island provide opportunities for many future use options.

Boat view from the south

Opposite: Aerial view from the north

Roseate tern

Sedge

SHARK ISLAND

Rock, 150 yards long, 590 yards east-southeast of Cabes Point, and 1/3 mile off northeast shore of St. Thomas Island. Several rocks, one 11 feet high, lie northeast. The name is translation of *Haye*, applied by the French and Dutch navigators; Spanish equivalent, *Tiburon*.

VEGETATIONAL AND FLORAL FEATURES
Many turkscap cactus grow on bare rock cliffs on the south and east sides of the island. Grasses and sedges grow on the flat crown and the northwest slope. Beach pea grows on the cliffs. Sea grape grows in the central saddle where protected from the wind.

Shark Island
Location	18° 20' 22" N
	64° 50' 40" W
Owner	V. I. Government
Acres	1.25 (.5 ha)
Elevation	32 ft. (9.7 m)
Shoreline	394 yds. (.36 km)

FAUNAL FEATURES
The crested anole is present. Roseate terns sporadically nest in numbers up to 1000 pairs. Zenaida doves and common ground doves nest on the rocks and in the grass. White-cheeked pintail duck nests have been found on the island.

GEOLOGICAL FEATURES
Shark Island offers no landing on the cobble beach due to shallow fire coral offshore; it is rocky and steep all around. The island is composed of a complex conglomerate cut by many dikes classified as Vr.

NEAR SHORE FEATURES
A submerged ledge is present off the south shore, attracting lobsters and nurse sharks. A shallow elkhorn coral reef extends toward St. Thomas to the west.

MANMADE FEATURES
None, but "egging" has been traditionally carried on.

RECOMMENDATIONS
Should be protected as a "no-entry" wildlife sanctuary.

Boat view from the east

Opposite: Aerial view from the east

Prickly pear tree
This treelike cactus can grow to 15 ft. in height. The edible fruits, which are reddish purple when ripe, are borne on the edges of the beavertail-like pads. The cactus can reproduce from the seeds in the fruits or will root vegetatively if a pad falls to the earth.

Green-backed heron

Little blue heron

STEVEN CAY

Cay, 350 yards long, 90 yards wide, .5 mile west of St. John Island in Pillsbury Sound. Probably same as *Shorbomanok* of earliest charts.

VEGETATIONAL AND FLORAL FEATURES
The low northern end of the island is covered with a dwarfed closed canopy dry tropical forest including *Acacia* and maho. The elevated southern end and detached rock are covered with grasses, sedges, and tree cactus.

FAUNAL FEATURES
The crested anole, barred anole, and dwarf gecko are present. The snowy egret, tricolored heron, little blue heron and green heron are all recorded as having nested here. Laughing gulls continue to nest on the southern point.

GEOLOGICAL FEATURES
The island is generally flat and covered with coral rubble except for a conglomerate bluff on the south end and an adjacent detached rock pinnacle with a quartz dike.

NEAR SHORE FEATURES
There is good snorkeling and diving all around but especially off the south and west sides. Heavy currents are present at times.

MANMADE FEATURES
A flashing white 4-second navigation light is maintained on the northwest point.

RECOMMENDATIONS
Continue to utilize as an unimproved recreation area since hurricane waves are likely to sweep the island.

Steven Cay
- **Location**: 18° 19' 55" N, 65° 48' 25" W
- **Owner**: V. I. Government
- **Acres**: 2.068 (.83 ha)
- **Elevation**: 32 ft. (9.7 m)
- **Shoreline**: 787 yds. (.72 km)

Boat view from the east

Opposite: Aerial view from the north

Boobies

The boobies (genus *Sula*) all feed by high-speed plunge diving to catch their aquatic prey. They all nest in groups on oceanic islands isolated from disturbance by man or terrestrial predators. Each species has a unique but broad repertoire of stereotyped behavior associated with mating and territory. Although the sexes are almost identical in appearance, the vocalizations are quite distinct.

Brown booby in flight

Masked booby

SULA CAY

Islet, severed by narrow cleft from southeast side of Cockroach Cay, northwest of St. Thomas. Danish *sule* and Spanish *sula*, booby, are from Icelandic *Sula, Gannet*; whence *Sula*, a genus of seabirds, including the boobies and gannet, *bassana*. These birds give name also to booby rock.

VEGETATIONAL AND FLORAL FEATURES
Wind-pruned sea grapes hold tenaciously to the bare rock on the center of the cay. Part of the peak plateau has patches of sedges.

Sula Cay
Location	18° 24' 11" N
	65° 03' 30" W
Owner	V. I. Government
Acres	1.9 (.76 ha)
Elevation	75 ft. (22.8 m)
Shoreline	501 yds. (.45 km)

FAUNAL FEATURES
The crested anole is present. Red-billed tropicbirds, brown boobies, masked boobies, Zenaida doves, and ground doves all nest here. Red-footed boobies are locally reported to have nested here prior to military bombardment.

GEOLOGICAL FEATURES
This is the southeastern tip of Cockroach Cay separated by a weathered-out dike. A second dike is in the process of weathering away to split Sula. Soil type is Vr with steep wave-swept cliffs.

NEAR SHORE FEATURES
Surrounded by deep water with large waves and strong currents.

MANMADE FEATURES
Military ordnance fragments are present.

RECOMMENDATIONS
Protect as an inviolate "no-entry" seabird breeding area.

Tabular basalt on the north point

Tyre palm

Opposite: Aerial view from the east

Copper outcrop on the northeast point

Fishing bat (echolocating)
The fishing bat typically roosts in dark rock clefts near the sea, but a colony existed for many years in the attic of Government House in Christiansted. A single young is born early in the spring and may be carried by the mother while foraging. Roosts of this bat can frequently be detected by the distinct penetrating odor. The bats have specialized long legs and toes with sharp claws, which enable them to catch fish swimming near the surface of the water. They may be observed fishing in many quiet bays at dusk where they use their sonar to locate the ripples caused by small fish at or near the water surfaces.

Cliffs

Thatch Cay

Island, 1 5/8 miles long, greatest width 760 yards, .5 mile from Eastend Quarter, north shore of St. Thomas Island. Names from growth of Teyer (sic) palms *Cocothrinax alta*, alternative names synonymous: Deck or Dek, Tatch. Teyer, Tyer, Touch, etc. Called *Cayo Verde*; alternative name "The Hope."

Vegetational and Floral Features
Dense tyre palm groves are present on the northern windward slopes. Most of the island is covered with dry forest which gives way to more open grass with *Acacia*, maran, and century plant areas on the southeast point.

Faunal Features
The common ground lizard, crested anole, grass anole, barred anole, dwarf gecko, and Puerto Rican racer are present. The whistling frog is also present, which is unusual for the cays. Goats and rats and most of the bird fauna of St. Thomas can be found. The first roseate terns of the yearly migration are often observed on the western point.

Geological Features
The island is composed of complex interactions of igneous and metamorphic rocks. Copper deposits are known. The north side has steep Vr cliffs while the south side slopes more gently to the sea with soil type CsF. The high peak is SgF. There are two small JuB areas on the south coast and a single salt pond on the southeast point. There are numerous rock clefts on the north side and a deep sea-level cave with bats.

Near Shore Features
Deep water borders the northern cliffs. Shallow water with corals occurs in the East Bay and Eva Bay. The northwest coast provides undersea caves and huge boulders for scuba diving.

Manmade Features
There is a stone house with a cistern on the southeast side near the salt pond. In earlier times the island was owned by the Knud Hansen family and had a working copper mine.

Recommendations
Encourage the removal of the goats.

Thatch Cay
- **Location** 18° 21' 42" N 64° 51' 30" W
- **Owner** Private
- **Acres** 237 (95.9 ha)
- **Elevation** 482 ft. (146 m)
- **Shoreline** 5.75 mi (9.25 km)

Opposite: Boat view from the east

Aerial view from the north

View with tyre palms

Land view from the west

Jamaican fruit-eating bat
Quite abundant throughout the Antilles, fruit bats serve as dispersal agents for many plants. The smaller seeds pass through the digestive tract undamaged. Fruits with larger seeds may be carried some distance before the bat stops at a convenient perch to consume the pulp and drop the seed. Roosts may be found in almost any dimly illuminated spot including the underside of dead palm fronds and in the central part of the dense crown of a tamarind tree. The conspicuous spear-shaped nose leaf is a useful feature in identifying this bat.

TRUNK CAY

Islet, 210 yards long, 80 yards from Trunk Bay beach, northwest shore St. John Island. Local name, superseding Peter's Cay; last confusing, as Peter Bay is 1/3 mile east, and Peter Island 8 miles east.

VEGETATIONAL AND FLORAL FEATURES
The vegetation on the higher parts of this cay is similar to that on the nearby mainland. Included are tyre palms, gumbo limbo, sea grape, *Acacia*, cacti, and grasses.

Trunk Cay

Location	18° 21' 27" N
	64° 46' 09" W
Owner	U. S. Government
Acres	1.04 (.42 ha)
Elevation	48 ft. (14.6 m)
Shoreline	525 yds. (480 km)

FAUNAL FEATURES
Rats and mice are present. The crested anole and barred anole have also been reported. Fruit bats feed on the island when ripe fruit is available.

GEOLOGICAL FEATURES
The majority of the cay is metamorphic conglomerate and sedimentary rock Vr, the highest part having CrE soils.

NEAR SHORE FEATURES
The National Park Service maintains a marked snorkeling trail on the southwest side. There is a shoal between the island and the beach.

MANMADE FEATURES
None.

RECOMMENDATIONS
Retain in present state.

Boat view from the east

Crab bush

Sooty tern
Sooty terns arrive in the Virgin Islands and roost in a colony in mid-April. The first eggs of the season are deposited on the ground in early May. An incubation period of 30 days is followed by a development period of about 8 weeks. The plumage of sooty terns is easily waterlogged, and they have great difficulty taking off if they land in the water. They feed offshore on small fish and squid, which are often caught in the air or near the water surface. These terns rarely swim and probably fly almost continuously except when near land for annual breeding. They leave the Virgin Islands by the end of September. Sooty terns can be distinguished from the similar bridled tern by the white stripe that stops over the eye.

Opposite: Aerial view from the north

Turtledove Cay

Rocky islet, 180 yards wide, lying 70 yards from north spit of Saba Cay, to which it is joined by a reef bare at extreme low water. Also called Turtledove Key, Dove Key, Turtle Dove Cay, from the bird so called, frequenting the islands, and variously known as *Cocotzin, Petit Tourterelle*, Dutch *Tortelduif*, Danish T*urtledue*, Latin *Turtur* or *Columba passerina*. Spanish equivalent, *Tortola*, but Spanish navigators called this cay *La Cucharacha* (The Cockroach).

Vegetational and Floral Features
The higher central part of the island is mostly grass and sedge covered. There is a fringe of wind-sheared sea grape on the north side. A dense stand of sea purslane grows on the upper parts of the beach. The thorny shrub crab bush is interspersed with other vegetation throughout the island.

Turtledove Cay
Location	18° 19' 00" N
	65° 00' 00" W
Owner	V. I. Government
Acres	3.73 (1.5 ha)
Elevation	50 ft. (15.2 m)
Shoreline	525 yds. (.48 km)

Faunal Features
Roseate terns, bridled terns, sooty terns, noddy terns, Zenaida doves, and common ground doves nest here. This is also the site of the largest laughing gull nesting population in the V. I. The crested anole, dwarf gecko, and Puerto Rican racer are present.

Geological Features
The shoreline is steep Vr except for a JuB beach on the south. A large fold in the lava can be seen on the east end. The more level top of the island is CrE.

Near Shore Features
A sandy shoal extends from the beach to nearby Saba Island. There is a very scenic shallow elkhorn coral reef to the east.

Manmade Features
Posted with wildlife management signs.

Recommendations
Maintain present status as an inviolate game preserve during nesting season from May through September.

Boat view from the west

Opposite:
Aerial from the east

Great blue heron

Royal tern

Sally lightfoot crab

Almost any patch of intertidal rocks in the Caribbean will be host to this ubiquitous crab. They are usually solitary and can walk forward and backward but always run sideways when hurried. While they seldom enter the water due to aquatic predators, they can swim very rapidly if necessary. They are extremely agile and feed by picking algae from the rocks in the wave break zone. When the larval crabs come ashore from the plankton, they have longer, thinner legs than the adults and look like a different species.

Two Brothers

Small barren twin rocks, with ledge on northeast, near center of Pillsbury Sound. Danish equivalent, *De To Brodre*; German, *Die Zwey Bruder*; Spanish, *Dos Hermanos*.

Vegetational and Floral Features
Sea grape, sedge, and buttonwood shrub maintain a precarious hold on the two largest rocks.

Two Brothers	
Location	18° 20' 19" N
	69° 49' 4" W
Owner	No record
Acres	.35 (.14 ha)
Elevation	10 ft. (3.05 m)
Shoreline	<1000 ft. (300 m)

Faunal Features
Seabirds including laughing gulls, roseate terns, red-billed tropicbirds, and royal terns have nested on the rocks in the past. Great blue herons favor this as a feeding site.

Geological Features
The entire outcrop is Vr.

Near Shore Features
The rocks are surrounded by reefs and shoals.

Manmade Features
A white 6-second navigation light is maintained on a steel skeleton tower.

Recommendations
Maintain in present condition as a popular dive site.

Boat view from the south

Southern Peninsula

African tulip

Opposite: Aerial view from the west

Red-footed tortoise
The red-footed tortoise was probably introduced to the Virgin Islands by pre-Columbian Indians as a food item during canoe voyages. The tortoise digs a shallow hole under a shady bush to deposit 3 to 5 eggs. After a 6-month incubation period, the young hatch and disperse, becoming sexually mature at about 4 years of age. They may reach a maximum length of 18 inches. They eat a great variety of leaves, fruits, flowers, and animal matter, and can survive extended periods with little food or water.

WATER ISLAND

Island, 3,240 yards long, 400 to 1,000 yards wide, lying off south shore of St. Thomas, from which Water Island is separated by Gregerie Channel. Equivalent names: Dutch, *Watereyland*; Danish, *Vando*; French, *Isle de l'Eau*; Spanish, *Isla del Agua*. Alternative name, *La Provindence*.

VEGETATIONAL AND FLORAL FEATURES
The vegetation is the same as that found on adjacent St. Thomas, including trees such as gumbo limbo, mampo, geiger, and the introduced African tulip.

FAUNAL FEATURES
The barred anole, crested anole, grass anole, common ground lizard, slipperyback skink, green iguana, and dwarf gecko are present. The Puerto Rican racer and the red-footed tortoise are common. Most of the birds nesting on St. Thomas also nest on Water Island with the addition of tropicbirds on the south-facing cliffs.

Water Island
Location	18° 19' 30" N
	64° 57' 00" W
Owner	U. S. Government
	(leased to a private corporation)
Acres	491.549 (198.9 ha)
Elevation	294 ft (89.37 m)
Shoreline	7.04 mi (11.32 km)

GEOLOGICAL FEATURES
Cliffs are present on the exposed south and east sides. Protected bays are present on the leeward side. There are four JuB beaches. The interior and higher elevations are CrE and CrF soil types. There are six salt ponds. The seventh and largest has been opened as a marina.

NEAR SHORE FEATURES
There are many shipwrecks on all sides of the island. Many coral reefs on all sides of the island provide scenic snorkeling and diving opportunities.

MANMADE FEATURES
Flamingo Bay and Pond have been dredged for use as a marina. Many houses, a hotel, roads, electrical lines, and water catchments are present.

RECOMMENDATIONS
The future status of the island and its lease is presently being debated by the federal and territorial governments. The undeveloped portions of the island could be maintained for public recreation and nature study areas.

Boat view from the south

Boat view from the north

Red-tailed hawk

Opposite: Aerial view from the south

WATERLEMON CAY

Islet, 250 yards west of Leinster Point, at east side of Leinster Bay entrance, northern shore of St. John. Called *Cayuelo Acantilado* (steep little cay), because of its bluff shore, except for a sand spit 80 yards southeast. Also, "Water Limon Kay" or "Waterlemon," from a plant there so called, the *Passiflora laurifolia*, which bears a bright yellow, finely flavored fruit, known as "bellapple." Chartmakers converted "Waterlemon" into the more familiar "Watermelon," this last translated by the Spanish into *Sandia* or *Zandia*. Local name, "Jewel Cay."

Waterlemon Cay
Location	18° 22' 09" N
	64° 43' 24" W
Owner	Private
Acres	.739 (.3 ha)
Elevation	25 ft. (7.6 m)
Shoreline	31 yds. (287 m)

VEGETATIONAL AND FLORAL FEATURES
The vegetation is unexpectedly varied for such a small cay. Woody trees and shrubs include gumbo limbo, mampo, caper, fish poison and sea grape. Smaller plants include prickly pear cactus (with edible fruits), jumping cactus, sea purslane, nicker bean and maran.

FAUNAL FEATURES
The crested anole and dwarf gecko are present along with rats.

GEOLOGICAL FEATURES
There is a JuB beach on the southeast point with the balance of the shoreline being Vr. The elevated central part of the island is CrE.

NEAR SHORE FEATURES
Shoals are present on the east, north, and south sides.

MANMADE FEATURES
None.

RECOMMENDATIONS
Purchase by National Park Service.

Sea grape and coconut trees

Boat view from the south

Zenaida dove

Beach pea
With buoyant salt-tolerant seeds giving rise to a tough, fast-growing, salt-resistant vine, this plant is a rapid colonizer of seasonally ephemeral beaches. The speckled seeds with a dark line around the perimeter appear regularly in the flotsam on tropical beaches.

Opposite: Aerial view from the north

WEST CAY

Double island, .5 mile long, 3/8 mile wide, lying northwest of Westend Point, St. Thomas. The northern hill has a double summit; the two segments are joined by a low sand-neck 50 yards across, forming the common beach of two coves, the southern of which affords a landing.

Vegetational and Floral Features

The sandy beach is bordered with beach pea and sea grape, with a small grove of coconut palms at the base of the upland. The uplands of both sections of the island are covered with a dry forest similar to the one found on adjacent St. Thomas.

West Cay
- **Location** 18° 21' 15" N
  65° 02' 51" W
- **Owner** V. I. Government
- **Acres** 40.308 (16.3 ha)
- **Elevation** 121 ft. (36.8 m)
- **Shoreline** 1.6 mi. (2.57 km)

Faunal Features

Deer and goats are present. Tropicbirds and doves nest here. Many of the other terrestrial birds from St. Thomas could be expected here. The crested anole, dwarf gecko, and Puerto Rican racer are present.

Geological Features

The island is nearly divided into two parts by a JuB beach over which the sea breaks frequently enough to prevent establishment of permanent vegetation. Most of the circumference is Vr. The crown of the larger easternmost part is CsF2 while the western peak is CsF.

Near Shore Features

West Cay is separated from Little St. Thomas by a small boat channel called Big Current Hole. The channel to the west, adjacent to Salt Cay, is narrow and not navigable.

Manmade Features

Frequently used as a campsite by local fishermen who have established semi-permanent fixtures.

Recommendations

Retain as a multiple-use recreation and wildlife management area.

Boat view from the southeast

Brown pelican
Brown pelicans are commonly seen throughout the Virgin Islands singly or flying in formation. They feed by plunging into dense schools of bait and engulfing several gallons of water containing fish in their widely opened bill and its distended pouch. Pelicans lay 2 to 3 eggs and nest in colonies on the tops of trees. Incubation is about 30 days with the chick flying at about 11 weeks. Injury and starvation are major sources of mortality as young birds learn to fish.

Boat view from the northwest

Opposite: Aerial view from the south

WHISTLING CAY

Cay, 640 yards long, 235 yards wide, 290 yards west of Mary Point, northern shore of St. John. Gravel beach at southeast point, where sailboats obtain cargoes of building gravel. Elsewhere, shore is precipitous; on north, cliffs rise to 130 feet. Name perhaps derived from Dutch *Wissel*, Danish *Vexel*, meaning "change"; or from Dutch *Baksel*, batch of baking, as of rolls or pottery, thought applicable to boulder pile on western point. Called by various cartographers: *Baxel, Boxel, Wessel, Wissel*; and by the Spanish, *Cayo Bajel.*

VEGETATIONAL AND FLORAL FEATURES

Most of the island is covered with a dry scrub forest including cacti, century plants, *Acacia*, gumbo limbo, and tyre palm.

FAUNAL FEATURES

Pelicans nest on the upper areas of the cay. Lizards are represented by the crested anole, the barred anole, and dwarf gecko. A green iguana was introduced in 1963.

GEOLOGICAL FEATURES

The periphery of the island is Vr with the exception of a southeast-facing JuB beach. The higher interior is soil type CsF.

NEAR SHORE FEATURES

There are many submerged rocks and ledges with some coral and gorgonian development.

MANMADE FEATURES

The old building which served as the port of entry into the U. S. Virgin Islands has been partly restored by the National Park Service.

RECOMMENDATIONS

Maintain as wildlife sanctuary with access allowed only to the south beach and the restored customs building.

Whistling Cay
Location 64° 45' 26" N
18° 22' 30" W
Owner U. S. Government
Acres 1.32 (.53 ha)
Elevation 202 ft. (61.4 m)
Shoreline 1444 yds. (1320 m)

Great blue heron

A young manglar

Manglars

Red mangrove seedling

Reddish egret

Great egret

Opposite:
Mature manglars

MANGLARS

VEGETATIONAL AND FLORAL FEATURES
Composed of red mangrove, they sometimes support epiphytic plants like vines, bromeliads, orchids, lichens, and mosses.

FAUNAL FEATURES
Manglars are used extensively as nesting and resting sites for herons, egrets, pelicans, white-crowned pigeons, hummingbirds, warblers, and other birds. Several species of anoles, iguanas, crabs, snails, and many other invertebrates also utilize them. They support a highly productive marine community. The fallen leaves are the basis for most food-chains in the nearby marine community. Lobsters and the reef-fish community are also dependent on them as nursery areas.

GEOLOGICAL FEATURES
The trees grow on silty/sandy bottoms, and the substrate never extends above the high-tide mark. There is no dry land associated with the manglars. Soil type is submerged-saturated (Ts).

NEAR SHORE FEATURES
Usually surrounded by turtle-grass flats and/or a mixed grass-algal community.

MANMADE FEATURES
Manglars are often used as a storm refuge for small boats, and in some areas fishing shacks or houseboats are moored to them or staked within them. They formerly provided frame material for planked boats.

RECOMMENDATIONS
Should remain as undisturbed fish and wildlife habitat except for emergency use during storms.

Manglars
Location	In shallow protected bays
Owner	V. I. Government
Acres	Usually < 1.0
Elevation	Sea level
Shoreline	No "shore"

White-crowned pigeon fledglings

White-crowned pigeons

White-crowned pigeon nest

Opposite: Ruth cay from the southeast

Man-made/Destroyed Islands

Vegetational and Floral Features
In the case of absolute destruction, such as that of Krause Cay in Krause Lagoon on St. Croix, the natural vegetation is complete obliterated and replaced by blacktop, concrete, or perhaps by a few planted ornamentals. On the dredge-spoil islands of St. Croix, grasses and sedges have become pioneers, followed by salt-resistant woody plants. Their chances of surviving a major hurricane are uncertain.

Faunal Features
No wildlife, except transitory birds, can be found where the cays were actually destroyed. On the spoil islands, resting shorebirds can be found, and some of them, such as killdeer, may occasionally nest there. Littoral animals such as crabs also utilize the spoil islands.

Man-Made/Destroyed Islands
Location Southshore St. Croix
Owner Various
Acres Sometimes extensive
Elevation A few feet above sea level
Shoreline Various

Geological Features
The geological-topographical features are completely destroyed along with the cay. The material of the spoil islands is that of the former sea bottom in the area of a shipping channel. This material has passed through the cutterheads of the dredge and was pumped through the hoses to its present site. In some cases, it is emplaced by a dragline bucket. Soil types - altered (Ma).

Near Shore Features
In the area of destruction, this may be either a "fill" or a dredged channel bottom or bulkhead. Water quality usually remains poor because of the continuing release of "fines" or industrial pollution. Careful management can mitigate these problems and return the area to some semblance of fish and wildlife habitats.

Manmade Features
Various.

Recommendations
Rehabilitate to control pollution and water quality and reduce noise by means of plantings and similar mechanisms for "naturalizing" an artificial environment.

Cow Rock

Yellow-crowned night heron

Calf Rock

Opposite:
Turtle Rock

UNVEGETATED ROCKS

VEGETATIONAL AND FLORAL FEATURES
Characterized by a lack of terrestrial vegetation, these rocks provide a habitat for marine algae at and below the waterline.

FAUNAL FEATURES
Utilized by marine organisms such as crabs and whelks. Seabirds use them as resting areas which are completely protected from terrestrial predators. Shorebirds such as herons and oystercatchers fish from them.

GEOLOGICAL FEATURES
Exposed and bare rock of such small area and low elevation that wave and spray action prevent the growth of terrestrial vegetation. Soil type Vr.

NEAR SHORE FEATURES
Sometimes surrounded by growing coral reefs which support a typical reef community.

MANMADE FEATURES
Sometimes used as a foundation for navigation lights. Many are named after ships or the captains of ships which foundered on them.

RECOMMENDATIONS
Maintain in undisturbed condition.

Unvegetated Rocks
(Many names)

Location	Mostly near islands or cays; some isolated
Owner	V. I. Government
Acres	Negligible
Elevation	A few feet
Shoreline	Negligible

Glossary of Place Names

The following glossary is composed of pertinent names and other information which have been extracted from "Geographic Dictionary of the Virgin Islands of the United States" by James William McGuire (U.S. Coast and Geodetic Survey, 1925). His references have been deleted and the scientific names of organisms have been modernized. These are the names he extracted from published material, including maps and charts. We have included all the names that we felt could become involved in questions or discussions regarding "rocks," "cays," and "islands." A few of these are names of submerged and/or nonvegetated rocks which are not otherwise discussed or treated here. The glossary provides a useful "cross-index" and source of information.

AGAY:
Aboriginal name of St. Croix Island; obtained by Christopher Columbus, who on November 14, 1493, approached St. Croix from the southward and is said to have entered Salt River Bay for frest water. Otherwise spelled *"Ayay."*

AGUA SALADA, ROCA DEL:
Spanish name of Saltwater-Money Rock.

ARRECIFE JOHNSON:
Spanish name of Johnson Reef, off northwest shore of St. John.

AWANGO ISLAND:
Lovango Cay.

AYAY:
Same as *Agay*, Indian name of St. Croix.

BAJEL:
Spanish spelling of Baxel, early name of Whistling Cay.

BAJO DEL AGUILA:
Spanish name of Eagle Shoal, St. John.

BALLAST ISLAND:
Islet near westernmost shore of St. Thomas Harbor: area 0.4 acres (no longer exists).

BARREL-OF-BEEF:
Rock cluster, bare 2 feet, 415 yards from shore, 1,210 yards southeast of Muhlenfels Point Lighthouse; east angle of Triangle Rocks.

BAXEL KAY:
Whistling Cay. Perhaps from Dutch *Baksel* (batch of rolls, baking of pottery) to which a boulder pile would bear a fancied resemblance.

BERGANTIN OR CARAVALLA, OR CARVEL:
Sail Rock in Virgin Passage. Spanish, *El Bergantin*.

BIG COCKROACH:
Same as Cockroach Cay.

BIG CURRENT HOLE:
Boat passage west of Little St. Thomas and the rock (42 feet high, area 0.64 acres) just north, and southeast of West Cay and its southeast reefs ending with a rock 2 feet high.

BIG FLAT CAY:
Islet, 213 yards long, 70 to 90 yards wide, area 2.9 acres, 1 1/2 miles southwest of Red Point, St. Thomas. North Knoll is 32 feet high. South Knoll, 26 feet high. Spanish name, *Cayo Raso*.

BIRD'S ISLAND, FUGLE-KLIPPEN:
Frenchman Cap.

BIRD'S KAY:
Frenchman Cap, or *Fugle-Klippen*. Also called "Bird's Key" or "Round Island."

BLAS, LAS ISLAS (DE):
Brass Islands.

BLAS GRANDE:
Spanish name of Inner Brass Island, meaning "Great Blas."

BLENDERS:
Ledge with 3 rocks awash, extending 50 yards west from Lizard Rock.

BLINDE KLIPPEN:
German, meaning "Blind (i.e., sunken) Rocks"; mistaken description of Triangle Rocks.

BLINDERS:
Rocks, awash at low tide, in Round Bay, 200 meters off point east of Elk Bay, eastern point of St. John.

Glossary of place names

BLUNDER ROCK:
5 feet high, area 0.6 acres; largest of Blunder Rocks, east of Lovango Cay.

BLUNDER ROCKS:
Cluster, dry and awash, 250 yards east- northeast of Lovango Point, 1 mile northwest of Hognest Point, St. John. Largest called Blunder Rock.

BOCKEN EYLAND:
Old Dutch name of Leduck Cay, St. John. *Bocken Eyland* is Dutch, meaning "Buck Island," near St. Croix. Originally *Pocken-Eyland*, q.v. By change of a single letter, *Pocken* (Guayaco) became *Bocken* (Buck); variously spelled *Boken, Bokken*, etc.; translated *Cabrite, Cabrito*, etc.

BOKEN-EYLAND:
Same as Buck Island, St. Thomas. Origin of name thus explained by Host: *Havde kun nogle saa vilde Gedebukker, som fromodentling have givit Anledning til Navnet.* "It had only a few quite wild buck goats, which probably have given rise to the name."

BOOBY ROCK:
Round islet 35 feet high, area 0.51 acre.

BORGEM, ISLITA:
Spanish name of LeDuck Cay, St. John. Referred to in the Derrotero as *La Islita Borgem, Isla Duck o Buck o Borgem*.

BOVONI CAY:
Covering nearly 50 acres.

BOXEL ISLAND:
Whistling Cay. See Baxel Cay.

BRAS ISLAND:
Same as Inner Brass.

BRASS ISLANDS:
Two considerable islands, known as Outer Brass and Inner Brass, each 3/4 mile long and 700 yards broad, with adjacent islets and rocks, 3 miles west of Hans- Lollik, off north shore of St. Thomas, 4 miles from its west end. Sometimes spelled "Blas," *Las Islas de Blas*.

CALF ROCK:
The easternmost rock of a pair called Cow and Calf, see Cow Rock.

CAYE GREEN:
Same as Green Cay, St. Thomas.

CAYO BAJEL:
Spanish name of Whistling Cay.

CAYO CONGO O LOVANGO CHICO:
Spanish name of Congo Cay.

CAYO CONSEJOS:
Spanish, meaning "Council Cay"; same as Flanagan Island.

CAYO FRANCES O DE AVES:
Spanish, meaning French or Bird Cay. Frenchcap.

CAYO PROTESTANTE:
Spanish name of Protestant Cay, St. Croix.

CAYO VERDE:
Spanish, "Green Cay"; same as Thatch Cay, also same as Green Cay.

CHACHA ROCKS:
Reef, with several other rocks awash; all forming a chain rising clear and steep from the depths, 330 yards east of Savana Islands. *Cadena de Rocas limpias*.

CHANNEL ROCK:
Awash, near center of reef extending east and west 5/8 mile in Buck Island Channel, 5/8 mile offshore north of Old Knight Estate, 1 3/4 miles west-northwest of East Point, St. Croix.

CINNAMON CAY:
Islet, 32 feet high, area 1.03 acres.

COCKROACH CAY:
Island, 151 feet high, 19 acres.

COCOLOBA CAY:
36 feet high, area 1.08 acres.

COCULUS ROCK:
Highest of a group of bare rocks, 400 yards east of Rotto Cay, off southeast shore of St. Thomas. Probably from *Kukeluse* or *Coculus*, an edible sea snail.

CONCHA, ROCA DE LA:
Spanish name of Welk or Whelk Rock.

CONGO CAY:
170 feet high, area 25.46 acres.

COW ROCK:
Islet, 10 feet high, lat. 18° x 18' 20", long. 64° x 50' 53", westernmost of cluster in southern approach to St. James Bay, 1/2 mile south of Deck Point. Sometimes referred to as "Cow," or "The Cow," (Spanish, *La Vaca*); or together with another rock 260 yards east, as "Cow and Calf." See Calf Rock.

CRAB ROCK:
Detached, inner of 2 rocks off east point of Camp Bay, Hans Lollik Island.

CRABE, ISLE À:
Saba Island, q.v. Spanish equivalents, *Cambaro, Cangrejo, Jaiba*.

CRICKET ROCK:
46 feet high, area 2.52 acres; steep pinnacled.

Glossary of Place Names

Cucaracha:
Spanish equivalent of Cockroach Cay; but name is rather confusingly applied to Turtledove Cay. See *La Cucaracha.*

Cucculus Key:
Same as Congo Cay.

Cuivre, Isle du:
Old French name of Inner Brass Island.

Current Hole:
Passage or Cut, 400 yards wide, bisected by Current Rock, between Water Point at east end of St. Thomas and northwest point of Great St. James. Also called "Current Passage," "Current Hole and Passage"; Spanish, *El Paso o Pasaje de la Corrient.* The eastern of the two channels was called by the Dutch *Passagie met klyne Vaartuygen.* Two other passages, at west end of St. Thomas are called, respectively, "Big Current Hole" and "Little Current Hole."

Current Rock:
13 feet high.

Deck Eyland:
Dutch name of Thatch Cay, northeast of St. Thomas. *Deck Eyland of Island Verde, Deck Eyland oder Verde,* both meaning "Deck Island" or "Green Island." Spanish, *Isla Verde.*

Deidrichs Cay:
Same as Buck Island, St. Croix. From Diedrichas Plantage, which occupied it in 1754.

Doerloo Cays:
Dutch phonetic equivalent of Danish *Duurloo,* name of colonial family from whom Durloe Bay and Cays took their name.

Dog Island:
Area 12.14 acres.

Dog-Island Cut:
Boat-passage, 440 yards wide, with 1 1/2-fathom rock in middle, between little St. James Island and Dog Island. *El Freu de la Isla del Perro.*

Dog Rock:
9 feet high, highest of group 200 yards east of Dog Island, south end of Pillsbury Sound. Spanish, *Piedra del Perro.*

Domkirk Rock:
Crag, with twin steeple-shaped pinnacles, resembling a cathedral, 100 yards southeast of Virgin Point, at south extremity of Savana Island. Danish *Domkirke,* or Dutch *Domkerk,* "Cathedral." Shows striking resemblance to views of Cathedrals at Rheims, Amiens, Tours, Notre Dame, Durham, Westminster, etc.

Dos Hermanos:
Spanish equivalent of Two Brothers.

Dove Key:
Turtledove Cay.

Drabanter:
Danish, meaning "Satellites," German, *Trabanten,* both applied to the cays adjacent to St. Thomas.

Dry Ledge:
Sandy islet, 100 meters long by 30 meters wide, area 4 square rods, 3 feet high, 500 yards off Richardsen Point, 1,000 yards west of Pull Point, north coast of St. Croix. Ground unstable; protected on north and east by coral reef.

Dry Rock:
2 feet high, 930 yards west-southwest (250° true) from Montalvan Point, Saba Cay. Nearby are two smaller rocks, a rock awash, reefs, and breakers. Called *Bank de Roches* (Bank of Rocks): *La roca que vela al sud de la Isla de Montalvan* ("the rock which covers at the south of the island of Montalvan"; namely, Saba), with mention of *Dos pequenas piedras que velan* ("two small rocks which appear").

Duck Cay:
Leduck Cay, St. John.

Duck Island:
Early name of Leduck Cay, St. John. *Peter le Ducks Eyland*; "Ducks Island"; "Duck Island"; "Duck Cay."

Durlo Cays:
Same as Durloe Cays.

Durloe Cays:
Three islets in northeast entrance to Pillsbury Sound, between Lovango Cay and Hog Nest Point, and 1 1/2 miles north-northeast of Cruz Bay, St. John. Named for a Hollander, Hans Doerloo. Islets severally named: Henly, Ramgoat, and Rata Cay.

Durloo Cays:
Same as Durloe Cays. *Durloos Kays.*

Durloos Kays:
Durloo or Dorloe Cays, St. John.

Dutch Cap:
Same as Dutchcap Cay.

Dutchcap Cay:
278 feet high, area 31.82 acres.

Dutchman Cap:
Same as Dutchcap Cay.

Dutchmancap:
Same as Dutchcap Cay.

Glossary of Place Names

Dutchman's Cap:
Same as Dutchcap Cay.

Eagle Shoal:
Two round coral patchs, with depths of 3 and 12 feet, 5/8 mile south of Leduck Cay and 1 mile east-northeast of Ram Head, St. John. Spanish, *Bajo del Aquila*.

El Bergantin:
Sail rock in Virgin Passage. *Penasco Llamado El Bergantin* ("a large rock called 'The Brigantine'").

Elephant Rock:
8 feet high, tallest and outermost off north point of Elephant Bay, northwest shore of Water Island. Lat. 18° x 19' 34.5" (1,060 m), Long. 64° x 57' 07.9" (233 m). Emanuel Cay: Bovoni Cay.

Ferfins Kay:
Perkins Cay, St. John.

Fish Cay:
Area 56 square rods, having an area of 13 square rods. See also Cocolaba.

Flamingo Rock:
5 feet high, 10 yards from shore, joined by low rocky neck to Flamingo Point, Water Island.

Flanagan Island:
Area 21.62 acres, 127 feet high.

Flat Cay:
Larger of Flat Cays. Also called Big Flat, Isla Plate, Plat, Flad, Raso.

Flatkeys:
Same as Flat Cays.

Flemingham:
Same as Flanagan Island.

Flemingham Cay:
Flanagan Island.

Flemish Cap:
Same as Dutchcap Cay, off St. Thomas Island.

Franske Seiler:
Sail Rock in Virgin Passage. Danish name meaning "French Sail."

Franskmandsklippen:
Danish, "Frenchman's Rock"; old name of Sail Rock.

Fransanns oder Vogel-Klippe:
Same as Frenchman Cap. ("A habitat of many thousand gulls and other birds, of whose savory eggs whole boatloads were carried away" [McGuire, 1925]).

Fransmanuar:
Alternative name of Carabella or Sail Rock. Probably a corruption of "French Man-O'-War."

Frauen Kay:
Same as Henley Cay; largest of three Durloe Cays, St. John.

Frederik Knoll:
Rocky patch, west side of harbor entrance, 2 or 3 fathoms, off Frederik Point, St. Thomas. Also called Frederiks Knoll; Spanish, *Bajos de Frederik*.

Frenchcap Cay:
183 feet above sea level, area 10.5 acres.

Frenchman's Cap:
Same as Frenchcap or Frenchman Cap.

Fugleklippen:
Same as Frenchman Cap. Also spelled *FugleKlippen* (Frenchman's Cap).

Fugleskjaerret:
Danish, meaning "Fowl-skerry" or "Bird Rock," with definite article; descriptive name of Frenchman's Cap or Frenchcap Cay. Also spelled *Fugleskjaer, Fugleskier*.

Galeota:
Spanish equivalent of French *La Galiote*, Sail Rock.

Galiota, Galiote, Galliot, La Galiote, etc:
Variant spellings of one of the names of Sail Rock.

Galiote, La:
Sail Rock, as called by early French mariners. Also *La Caravelle, Le Hue*.

Gedeoen:
Danish equivalent of Buck Island, St. Croix.

Goat Island:
Same as Buck Island, St. Croix. Also called *Boken, Bocken, Bokken, Pocken; Cabrit, Cabrite, Cabrito; Vert*, etc.

Goat Rock:
Outstanding boulder, 10 yards from small rocky neck forming main angle of southwest shore of Little Hans Lollik Island.

Goldring Rock:
Local name of Packet Rock.

Gorret Rock:
Bare 2 feet, with rock awash nearby, 100 yards off southwest point of Dutchcap Cay, lat. 18° x 22' 48", long. 65° x 03' 52". Spanish *Gorrete* (small cap), *Roca Seca* (dry rock).

Gorro Flamenco:
Spanish name of Dutchcap or Dutchman's Cap; from *Gorro* (cap or coif) and *Flamenco* (Flemish); hence, "Flemish Cap."

Glossary of place names

Graes-Kaien:
Alternative of *Bokken Eiland* (Buck Island); "a small island between *Fugleskiaeret* (French cap) and St. Thomas."

Graes Kay:
Danish name of Grass Cay, near St. Thomas.

Grand St. James:
Great St. James Island.

Grasklip Point:
Detached islet 40 feet high, area 0.89 acres, at southeast end of Outer Brass Island, lat. 18° x 23' 41.4" (1,273 m), long. 64° x 58' 03.4" (100 m). Same as Grass Point or Gras Point.

Gras Point:
Same as Grasklip Point.

Grass Cay:
230 feet high, area 48.8 acres or 49.3 acres.

Great St. James:
Island, area 156.9 acres, highest summit 175 feet.

Green Cay:
24 feet high, area 128 square rods.

Green Cay:
Area 12.77 acres.

Green Island:
Alternative name of Savana Island.

Green Kay:
Same as Green Cay, Island, and Estate.

Groen Eyland:
Same as Green Cay, St. Thomas.

Grøn Kay:
Same as Green Cay Estate St. Croix.

Grønkayen:
Green Cay, St. Croix; Danish name with article.

Groot St. Jems:
Great St. James Island.

Gross Hans Lolk:
Hans-Lollik Island.

Gross St. James:
German name of Great St. James Island which, in 1777, had a cotton plantation.

Grosz Hanloik:
Same as Hans Lollik Cay.

Ground Rock:
Detached, bare 1 foot, near east point of Hans Lollik Island. Lat. 18° x 23' (1,432 m), long. 64° x 53' (1,754 m).

Grunkey:
German name of Green Cay, St. Croix.

Hanseatic Rock:
Same as Hans-Lollik Rock.

Hanslolk:
Same as Hans-Lollik Island; Klein Hans Lolk and Gross Hans Lolk, name of the islands severally.

Hans-Lollik Island:
743 feet high, area 480.2 acres.

Hans-Lollik Islands:
Group, consisting of Hans-Lollik Island (proper), Little Hans-Lollik, Pelican Cay, and Hans-Lollik Rock; lying 2 miles off middle of north shore of St. Thomas. Spanish, *las Islas de Hans-Lollik*.

Hans Lollik Rock:
200 yards across, awash, always breaking, 700 yards southeast of south end of Hans-Lollik Island. (Not *Hanslollik, Hanslolk, Hanseatic, Hans-netik*, nor White Horse).

Hansnetik:
Island, same as Hans-Lollik.

Hassel Island:
Forms the western side of St. Thomas Harbor. Also known as Orkanshullet Island.

Haye England:
Same as Shark Island. Probably early confusion of this with Turtleback Rock to northwest seems to have caused a shifting of all coastal names thence around to Beverhout Point, St. Thomas.

Henley Cay:
Largest of three Durloe Cays, off northwestern coast of St. John. (Not *Frauen*.)

Heu, Le:
French, meaning "The Hoy"; one of three names applied to Sail Rock, the others being *Caravelle* and *Galiote*. Spanish equivalents: *Hoya, Caraba, Galeota*.

Hognest Rock:
25 feet high, 55 yards long, close inshore, just north of Hognest Point, St. John.

Holm Buck Island:
Danish, *Holm*, signifying "Islet" or "Cay." Buck Island, off St. Croix.

Hope Cay:
Mentioned in Virgin Islands Recorders Office (AED). See Thatch Cay. (Not from McGuire.)

Hoy:
Sail Rock, also called *Bergantin, Carvell*, etc. French, *Heu*;

Glossary of Place Names

Spanish, *Hoya*. The multiplicity of names long applied to this islet all in common signify a kind of sailing vessel.

Hoya:
Spanish, with article *La Hoya*, equivalent to English "Hoy," French *Heu*; same as Sail Rock.

Hunde Eyland:
Dog Island.

Hunde Island:
Islet east-southeast of Little St. James Island; same as Dog Island.

Hund Eyland:
Original Dutch name of Dog Island, with same meaning.

Ile Verte:
French, "Green Isle," properly same as Green Cay, St. Croix, though transferred to Buck Island.

Inner Brass Island:
256 feet high, area 128 acres, uninhabited.

Inside Brass:
Inner Brass Island.

Isla Broken o Buck:
Buck Island, near St. Thomas.

Isla Chica de Hans Lollik:
Spanish name of Little Hans-Lollik Island.

Isla del Agua:
Spanish equivalent of Water Island.

Isla Grande de Hans Lollik:
Spanish name of (Great) Hans-Lollik Island.

Isla Gras:
Spanish name of Grass Cay.

Isle à Cabrit:
Buck Island, St. Croix. See *Isle Vert*.

Isle à Crabe ou Petit Isle de Saba:
French, "Crab Island, or "Little Saba Island"; early name of Saba Cay.

Isle Bokken:
Buck Island.

Isle de L'Eau:
French equivalent of Water Island.

Isle de Savane:
French name of Savana Island.

Isle du Sabbat:
Saba Cay. See *Isle à Crabe*, etc.

Isle Hay:
French name of Shark Island.

Isle Plate:
French name of Flat Key.

Isle Rouge:
French name of Rotto Cay.

Islet Rond et Birds Kay ou Caye des Oiseaux:
Frenchcap Cay.

Isle Vert:
French, meaning "Green Island"; not, however, applied to Green Cay but to Buck Island, St. Croix. Doubtless from the pristine density of the Guayaco or Pokholt forest growth, now disappeared.

Islote de Montalvan:
Spanish name of Saba Cay.

Jack Rock:
Largest cluster of rocks off point separating Vessup Bay from Muller Bay, St. Thomas. G.P., lat. 18° x 19' 38" (1,165 m), long. 64° x 50' 53" (1,550 m).

James Islands:
Group, composed of Great and Little St. James, and Hunde or Dog Island.

Jewel Cay:
Present local name of Waterlemon Cay, St. John.

Johnson Reef:
1/2 mile long, from Freeze Bay to 1/4 mile north of Lagoon Point, on western side of Coral Bay, St. John Island; composed of coral heads, bare at low water, and always breaking.

Johnson Reef:
Coral formation, 200 yards broad by 1/4 mile long; shoal area, about 100 by 160 yards, always breaking; 1/2 mile from northwest coast of St. John, midway between Durloe Cay and Whistling Cay. Summit of a shoal extending from shore northwest 1,600 yards. Arrecife Johnson.

Kakerlak:
Danish equivalent of Cockroach Cay. Also spelled *Kakkerlak* or *Kakelak*; hence, Creole, *Kakelaka*.

Kalkoen Eylandt:
Dutch equivalent of Kalkun Cay.

Kalkun Cay:
73 feet high, area 3.53 acres, or, including "Vogelklip" at south end, 3.61 acres, lat. 18° x 21' 09.8" (300 m), long. 65° x 03' 25.8" (879 m).

Glossary of Place Names

Kalkunisland:
Variant form of name, Kalkun Cay.

Kalkun, Kalkunoe:
Variant form of name, Kalkun Cay.

Karavelle:
Sail Rock

Kastel Reef:
Off Kastel Point, north shore of St. Thomas. *Kasteel*, in Dutch meaning "Castle"; *Kasseel*.

Kees Eyland:
Early Dutch name of Cas Cay.

Kid Rock:
20 square rods in area, near eastern shore of Capella Bay, just south of passage between Capella Cays.

Klein Hans Lolk:
Little Hans Lollik I.

Klein Saba oder Sabbath:
German, "Little Saba or Sabbath," i.e., Saba Cay.

Klein St. James:
German equivalent of Little St. James I.

Klipper:
Name of Carval or Carbela Rock. Dutch, *Klipper Klip* (Clipper Rock).

Klyn Eyland:
Dutch, meaning "small island"; descriptive term applied to Range Cay, St. Thomas.

Klyn Sabbath, 't Eyland:
Dutch, "the Island Little Sabbath" same as Saba Cay.

Klyn St. Jems:
Early Dutch name of Little St. James I.

Klyn S. Thomas oder Savanneyland:
Savana Island.

Krause Lagoon:
Area of shallow pools, channels, mud banks, and mangrove islets, 1 5/8 miles long, occupying angular embayment, enclosed behind narrow barrier of Krause Peninsula and Cay and Anguilla Point, south coast of St. Croix. Named for Obrist-Lieutenant Krause, of whose estate (Caramaw Hall) this was part. Less correctly spelled *Krausse* or *Krusse*. Also called Anguilla Pond, *Kongens Lagune*. (No longer exists.)

Kuglen:
Danish, "the cone": early name of Whitehorse Rock, near Saltriver Point, St. Croix.

Kukelusse Kai or Kay:
Same as Congo Cay.

Kukkelusse:
Congo Cay, St. John.

La Caravelle, La Galiote, Le Heu:
Sail Rock in Virgin Passage. English equivalents: The Caravel, the Galliot, the Hoy. Compared to Corvette, or Brigantin.

La Cucaracha:
Spanish name of Turtledove Cay.

La Galiote:
French, "The Galliot" or "Bark"; alternative name of Sail Rock.

Lagarto, El Islote:
Spanish name of Lizard Rock.

Lagoon Mangrove:
Several small manglars or mangrove clumps, covering about 300 square rods in southeast portion of Mangrove Lagoon.

La Isla Cabrito, O Savana:
Spanish name of Savana I.

Lang Bank:
Remarkable hook-shaped, wall-sided, narrow coral ledge, marked by dangerous breakers in heavy weather; extending from 3 to 10 miles northeast of East Point, St. Croix. Depth, 6 to 10 fathoms; width, 1/2 to 1 mile; length around hook, 9 miles; recurving toward similar coral wall at southern edge of soundings inside 100-fathom curve which extends southwest 6 miles further and terminates 2 miles south of East Point, having depths of 8 to 10 fathoms and width of 100 to 600 yards. Total width of soundings, 3 to 5 miles.

La Piedra del Scorpion o Alacran:
Spanish name of Scorpion Rock.

La Provindence:
Alternative or parenthetic name for Water Island; from a plantation so called, which left its name on Providence Point.

La Roca de Hans-Lollik:
Spanish name of Hans-Lollik Rock.

La Roca Carvela:
Spanish "Caravel Rock," same as Sail Rock.

Lavango Cay:
Variant spelling of Lovango Cay.

Leduck Cay:
84 feet high, area 13.52 acres (with adjacent rocks, 0.55 acre additional). Perhaps same as Leduck. Lat. 18° x 19' 03.4" (105 m), long. 64° x 41' 15.2" (446 m).

Glossary of place names

Lee Rock:
16 feet high, area 0.24 acre, close to Lee Point at western extremity of Thatch Cay (not West Rock).

Le Heu:
French, "The Hoy" alternative name of Sail Rock.

Levango Kay:
Lovango Cay.

Lille Hanslollik:
Danish name of Little Hans-Lollik I.

Lille James Eyland:
Little St. James Island, near St. Thomas.

Lille St. James:
Danish name of Little St. James I.

Lille Saba:
Danish name of Saba Cay or Little Saba Island.

Limestone Rock:
4 feet high, outer and smaller of twin rocks, on extensive coral reef 175 yards long, 120 and 160 yards, respectively, south of Carol Point, Water Island.

Little Cockroach:
Cricket Rock.

Little Current Hole:
Boat passage, 30 yards wide, between Little St. Thomas and West Cay.

Little Flat Cay:
Bare rock, 11 feet high, 55 yards wide, area 60 square rods; 80 yards northeast of (Big) Flat Cay. Spanish equivalent *Rasito*; also *Vogel Eyland*.

Little Green Key:
Same as Green Cay, St. Croix - St. Thomas.

Little Hans-Lollik:
217 feet high, area 100.48 acres, to which add 19 square rods for steep rock on east and 140 square rods for ledge awash on northeast.

Little Saba:
Saba or Montalvan Cay. In contradistinction to Saba Island, 110 miles east-southeast, belonging to Holland.

Little St. James:
142 feet high, area 68.73 acres, "James," lat. 18° x 18' 06.25" (192 m); long. 64° x 49' 37" (1,088 m); summit of island.

Little St. Thomas:
Low grassy peninsula, almost an islet, with two knolls of 21 and 50 feet, joined by a tombola to the west end of St. Thomas. Longitude of western extremity 65° x 02' 32". Spanish, *San Tomas Chico*. Not to be confused with West Cay. See also Lille St. Thomas Bay.

Lizard Rock:
Steep, rugged islet, 14 feet high, area 0.21 acres, lat. 18° x 23' 15" (460 m), long. 64° x 59' 24" (831 m), 1,700 yards west of Inner Brass Island and 1,530 yards north of Vluck Point, St. Thomas. Miscalled "Cricket." Spanish, *El Islote Lizard o Lagarto*. Danish equivalent, *Firben* (not on charts). Sometimes, simply (The) "Lizard." See Lizard Rocks.

Lizard Rocks:
Group of 6 bare rocks; the largest, called Lizard or Lagarto Rock; with 3 rocks awash, 50 yards west, called Blenders.

Loango:
Lovango Cay. Name of district on west coast of Africa, 50 miles north of river Congo, also applied to coast northward to Equator; whence doubtless slaves were imported into West Indies. The slight change of orthography established serves as a useful distinction.

Lodsø:
Danish, "Pilot Island"; alternative of Protestant Cay.

Lomo Tortuga:
Spanish name of Turtleback Rock.

Long Reef:
1 1/2 miles long, about 3/4 miles off southern shore of St. Croix, opposite Krause Point, enclosing a good anchorage.

Long Reef:
Narrow bar, stretching from Princess Plain eastward 2 miles; eastern end enclosing western side of Christiansted Harbor entrance, St. Croix. Spots nearly awash; on Danish charts, noted as *tildel tørt* (partly dry). Danish name, *Lange-Rev*.

Loots Kay:
Obsolete Dutch name of Protestant Cay, St. Croix. Properly, Loods Kay. *Loots* signifies "shed"; *Loods*, "Pilot."

Lootskey:
Alternative name of Protestant Cay, St. Croix.

Los Dos Santiagos:
Spanish, meaning "The Two Saints James"; name of the St. James Islands.

Los Triangulos:
Spanish, meaning "The Triangles" or (better) Triangle Rocks.

Lotskeyen:
Protestant Cay, *sonm og kaldes, Lotskayen* (which also is called "the Lods Cay").

Lovango Cay:
Area 117 5/6 acres, height of hill at east end, 247 feet; at west end, 255 feet. Crescentic bight, 0.25 mile wide on south shore; several houses along beach. Population 20; public school opened, 1917.

Glossary of Place Names

Lovango Cays:
Three Islands, viz., Lovango, Congo, and Mingo Cays, administratively attached to Cruz-Bay Quarter, St. John. Called by the Spanish, respectively, *Lovango Grande, Chico,* and *Medio.*

Lovango Chico:
Same as Congo Bay.

Lovango Grande:
Spanish, "Great Lovango," same as Lovango Cay; thus distinguished from *Lovango Chico,* "Little Lovango," now Congo Cay, and from *Lovango Medio,* "Middle Lovango," now Mingo Cay.

Lovango Medio:
Mingo Cay.

Machuto-Freyyet:
Cas Cay, so named on early unidentified map.

May Point:
Triangulation station on sharp bluff, 28 feet high, at south end of Steven Cay, formerly known as Steven May. Lat. 18° x 19' 50.3" (1,516.3 m); long. 64° x 48' 26.545" (779.54 m). Just off the point is a rock 31 feet high, area 0.12 acres.

Meeren Cay:
Old name of Steven Cay, in Pillsbury Sound near St. John. Shorter form, *Meren*; dubiously, *Meeven.*

Meeven Cay:
Same as, and probably an engraver's error for, *Meeren Cay,* now called Steven Cay.

Mercy Key:
Meren Key, now Steven Cay. In script, either Mercy or Meren might be misread for the other.

Meren Key:
Variant of Meeren Cay, now Steven Cay. See Mercy Key.

Midway Rock:
Large detached shore rock, just off rocky point; lat. 18° x 18' (1,187 m); long. 64° x 53' (256 m).

Mingo Cay:
186 feet high, area 48.35 acres.

Mingo Klippe:
Mingo Rock.

Mingo Rock:
Breaker rock, awash at low water, 175 yards west-southwest of Moravian Point, western extremity of St. John. *Mingo Klippe.*

Montalvan:
Spanish name of Saba Cay, *La Isla de Montalvan,* also *El Islote de Montalvan.*

Mouton:
Coral reef, extending south from Southwest Point of St. Croix for 1 1/4 miles. Named on old French charts *Le Mouton* (the sheep), the foaming waves resembling white wool.

Murder Rock:
Islet, area 0.09 acres, near southern shore of Lovango Cay. Spanish, *Roca del Asesino.*

Narrows:
Generic term, designating passage between Great Thatch Island (Br.) and northern shore of St. John Island. Also called "The Narrows." Danish equivalent, *Snaevring.* To avoid ambiguity of circumlocution, herein sometimes designated as "Thatch Narrows," although the rather similar name, "Thatch Island Cut," is applied to a smaller pass connecting on the north.

Newfound Bay:
Indentation nearly 400 yards wide, between coral reefs on north shore of Eastend Peninsula, 2/3 mile northwest of Eastend Point, St. John. "Rock" is a lone rock, 10 feet high, at edge of coral and gravel beach, at origin of a coral reef, southeast shore of bay; lat. 18° x 20' 50.7" (1,559 m), long. 64° x 40' 3.2" (98 m). See Sibbe Bay.

Nordoe:
Danish, *Nordø* (North Island); same as Pelican Cay, most northerly islet of Danish West Indies.

Northside Rocks:
Shore rocks fringing a jagged low bluff, where coast of St. Croix bends at Northside Estate. See Point Sous-le-Vent.

Oiseaux, Caye Des:
French, "Cay of the Birds" or "Bird Cay," equivalent to Dutch *Vogelklip* and applied to any rocky islet providing a nesting place for seabirds. Given as name of (1) French Cap, (2) Grass Cay.

Økajaede:
Danish, "island-chain"; as, that formed by Thatch, Grass, Mingo, and Lovango Cays; one of two "*Øraekker*" north of St. John.

Oostent-Punt:
Dutch name, meaning "Eastend Point"; French, *Pointe de l'Este*; Danish, *Ostende Pent*; on early maps, applied to most prominent salient between *de Koks punt* (Coki Point) and *Roodehoek* (Redhook Point), hence identifies with Cabes Point, St. Thomas. Now so accepted and established, as evidenced by bounds of Eastend Quarter. Striking similarity of configuration between (1) Coki and Footer Point with Turtleback Rock and (2) Cabes and Prettyklip Points with Haye or Shark Island produced confusion and shift of names of Points and Bays all the way from Coki Point to Jersey Bay. *Oostent Punt,* being south of *Haye* (Shark Island), doubtless

Glossary of Place Names

was originally intended to designate present Redhook Point, while latter name more appropriately belonged to present Cabrita Point, which is in fact a "red hook." Contrary usage now fixed.

ORKANSHULLET ISLAND:
Same as Hassel Island.

ORNEN ROCK:
Sunken danger to navigation. Shoal spot, depth 9 feet, on dangerous reef, 1 mile east of Inner Brass Island and 1/2 mile northwest of Picaro Point, St. Thomas. Danish, *Ørnen*, the Eagle; Spanish, *Roco Ornen*.

ØRNEN:
Danish, meaning "the Eagle"; Ørnen Rock.

OUTER BRASS:
412 feet high, area 108 acres, exclusive of Grasklip Cay, 61 square rods; overgrown with teyer (sic) palms and brush.

OUTSIDE BRAS:
Outer Brass Island.

OUTSIDE BRASS:
Outer Brass Island.

PACKET ROCK:
Coral reef, 100 yards in extent, least depth 5 feet, 2,520 yards north of Buck Island Lighthouse, 1,600 yards 256° from Long Point, 58 mile off south coast of St. Thomas. *La Roca del Paquete*, *Roches Sous-l'Eau* (rocks underwater); alternative name, "The Goldring."

PAIS-PERDU:
French, meaning "lost land"; specifically applied to the "manglar" (mangrove-island) enclosing Krause Lagoon, St. Croix, on the South. See Krause Point.

PATRICIA CAY:
Area 33.4 acres.

PELICAN CAY:
19 feet high, area 4.5 acres; low, rocky. Latitude of north point, 18° x 25' 02.36".

PELICAN ROCK:
Detached shore-rock, 10 feet high, west of Pelican Cay; lat. 18° x 25', long. 64° x 55' 37".

PELICAN ROCK:
7 feet high, jagged with many pinnacles; highest of group of rocks, bare and awash, 90 yards off south entrance point of Hanson Bay, Coral Bay, St. John. Local name.

PERKINS CAY:
Area 0.56 acres. Lat. 18° x 21' 22" (674 m), long. 64° x 46' 39.48" (1,159 m).

PERRO, ISLA DEL:
Spanish name of Dog Island, near St. Thomas.

PERRO, PIEDRA DEL:
Spanish name of Dog Rock near Dog Island.

PESCADO, CAYO:
Spanish equivalent of Fish Cay, St. John.

PETER LE DUCKS EYLAND:
Peter Leduck's Island, earliest name of Leduck Cay, Coral Bay, St. John.

PETER'S CAY:
Same as Trunk Cay, St. John.

PETER'S KAY:
Trunk Cay, St. John.

PETIT S. JAMES:
French for "Little St. James" Island.

PIEDRA CUBIERTA:
Spanish, meaning "Covered Rock," applied to danger shown by Spanish and Danish, but not English, charts. Situated 300 yards south of Gorret Rock, which is 100 yards off southwest point of *El Garro Flamenco* or Dutchcap Cay.

PIEDRA DEL PERRO:
Spanish name of Dog Rock.

PIEDRA DEL SCORPION:
Spanish name of Scorpion Rock.

PIEDRA DE PUNTA SANDY:
Spanish, Sandy Point Rock.

PIEDRA DE RUPERTO:
Spanish name of Rupert Rock.

PIEDRAS SUELTAS:
Spanish, meaning "loose or scattered rocks," applied to a reef over which the sea usually breaks. They lie from 100 to 300 yards off Virgin Point, southwest end of Savana Island.

PLAT EYLAND:
Dutch name of Flat Cay.

PLATE, ISLE:
French name of Flat Cay.

POCKEN-EYLAND:
Original Dutch name of Buck Island, St. Croix. The tree with which the island, now an arid waste, was forested was the *Guaiacum officinale*. Synonym: Wayako, Guayaco, Guyacan, Guaiac, Lodonero, Lignumvitae, Lignumsanctum, Pokhout, Pokkenholt, Indianwood, *et supra*.

Glossary of place names

Pockeneyland:
Same as Buck Island, near St. Croix.

Pokkeneyland:
Danish form of Dutch name of Buck Island, St. Croix (which got its name from the pokholt tree, with which it was once overgrown).

Porpoise Rocks:
Shallow ledge in southern approach to West Gregerie Channel, 3/4 to 1 mile west of Flamingo Point, Water Island, and 1 1/2 miles south of Red Point, St. Thomas. Consists of two connected breaker-reefs 1/4 mile apart: northeastern reef nearly 200 yards wide, showing 2 bare rocks, largest 3 feet high, others awash or sunken; southwestern reef, 30 yards wide, with rock bare 2 feet. Also called "Porpoises"; Spanish, *Las Rocas del Puerco Marino*; Dutch, *Zeearken*; Danish, *Marsvin*.

Porpoises:
Porpoise Rocks.

Prinds Roberts Klippe:
Danish name of Rupert Rock in St. Thomas Harbor. Also spelled *Prinds Ruperts, Prins Robberts Klip, Prinz Robert Klippe*.

Prinds Rupert:
Same as Rupert Rock, St. Thomas.

Prins Robberts Klip:
Dutch name of Prince Rupert Rock, now simply Rupert Rock.

Printz-Roberts Klippe:
Rupert Rock.

Prinz Roberts Klippe:
Rupert Rock in St. Thomas Harbor.

Protestant Cay:
38 feet high, area 3.94 acres. Composed of conglomerate consisting of well-waterworn bluebeach pebbles, embedded in calcareous mud. Three-foot reef extends northwest 270 yards. Site of Fort Sofia Frederika, also of large cistern.

Protestant-Kai:
Danish, same as Protestant Cay, St. Croix.

Protestankaien:
Danish, "The Protestant Cay," St. Croix.

Protestantkey:
Variant of Protestant Cay, St. Croix; in German, *Protestantkey oder Lootskey* and in Danish, *Protestantkeye, som og kaldes Lotskeyen* (which is also called Lots Cay).

Puerco Marino, Las Rocas del:
Spanish name of Porpoise Rocks, south of St. Thomas.

Pull Rock:
6 feet high, detached shore rock off northern end of Pull Point, north coast of St. Croix.

Ramgoat Cay:
30 feet high, area 2.7 acres.

Ram Goat Cay:
Error for Ramgoat Cay.

Range Cay:
Islet, 21 feet high, area 0.46 acres, close inshore southeast of Brewers Bay; 1,360 yards northwest of Red Point, Southside Quarter, called *Klyn Eyland* (Little Island) by Van Keulen. Present name proposed by "this being on the end of a range for a submarine trial course." Islet connected with mainland at low water by narrow strip of sand and coral.

Rasos, Cayos:
Spanish name of Flat Cays.

Rata Cay:
15 feet high, area 0.51 acres, with 2 or 3 rocks close inshore.

Ratta Cay:
Same as Rata Cay.

Red Point Shoal:
Reef, least depth 2 to 4 feet, 612 yards south-southwest of Red Point, St. Thomas. At 255 yards from Point is a ledge awash and at 122 yards a bare rock 7 feet high, in lat. 18° x 19' 49", long. 64° x 58' 23". Spanish, *Restinga de la Punta Roja*.

Roca Carval o Caravela:
Spanish name of Carval or Carabela Rock, near Congo Cay.

Roca de la Concha:
Spanish name of Welk Rock.

Roca del Agua Salada:
Spanish name of Saltwater Money Rock.

Roca del Asesino:
Spanish name of Murder Rock.

Roca del Paquete:
Spanish name of Packet Rock.

Roca Ornen:
Spanish name of Ornen Rock.

Rocas del Puerco Marino:
Spanish name of Porpoise Rocks.

Rocas Limpias:
Spanish, meaning "clear rocks," descriptive of chain of clear steep rocks showing along a reef 330 yards east of Savana Island.

Glossary of place names

Roches Sous-l'Eau:
French, meaning "submerged rocks"; applied to Packet Rock.

Rondomlelyk:
Old name of Outer Brass Island, perhaps also its 412-foot summit. Dutch *Rondom* (roundabout, all around), *de* (not *le*, the), *lyk* (modern *lijk*, corpse), hence "all around the corpse"! Local residents informed the author that this was once a "treasure island," resorted to by pirates, who here buried their dead and hid their booty in a large cave from which Cave Cove takes its name.

Roode Eyland:
Dutch name of Rotto Cay.

Rotto Cay:
83 feet high, area 2 acres, covered with scrub.

Rotto Key:
Same as Rotto Cay.

Round Key:
Same as Rotto Cay.

Round Reef:
Coral patch, 400 yards in diameter, with dry spot 3/8 mile west-northwest of Fort Louise Augusta, Christainsted Harbor entrance, St. Croix. On Danish charts, called *Runde-Rev*.

Runde-Rev:
Same as Round Reef, St. Croix.

Rupert Rock:
Islet, 12 feet high, area 0.31 acres, top whitewashed; 400 yards south-southwest of Havensight Point, 1/2 north of Muhlenfels Point Lighthouse, at narrowest part of St. Thomas Harbor entrance channel; with boulders just covered at high water extending 50 to 100 yards west. Spanish, *La Piedra de Ruperto*. Formerly called Prince Rupert's Rock; Danish, *Prinds Roberts Klippe*, etc.

Saba Cay:
202 feet high, area 30.3 acres. Lat. 18° x 18' 23" (710.8 m), long. 65° x 00' 08" (234.6 m).

Sabbat, Isle du:
Saba Cay.

Sail Rock:
125 feet high. Resort of seabirds. Six-inch shells scattered over the island. A tankhouse was built in cavern, concrete platform on crag, and acetylene light established, 150 candlepower, flashing white, visible 9 miles.

Saint James:
Same as Great St. James.

Saint James Islands:
Group off east end of St. Thomas Island composed of Great St. James, Little St. James, Dog Island, Fish Cay, and some rocky islets. Called by the Spanish *Los Dos Santiagos*.

Salt Cay:
242 feet high, area 55.82 acres.

Saltcay Passage:
Nearly 1 mile wide, between Dutchcap and Salt Cay; depths 13 to 19 fathoms, clear of dangers except a covered rock, 325 yards southwest of Dutchcap Cay. Local name.

Saltkey:
Salt Cay.

Saltvandpenge:
Danish equivalent for Saltwater-Money (Rock).

Saltwater-Money Rock:
Islet, 8 feet high, area 2,700 square feet, 0.5 mile southeast of Kalkun Cay and 5/8 mile southwest of West End of St. Thomas. Spanish, *Roca del Agua Salada*.

Sandboard Shoal:
Reef in Christiansted Harbor, St. Croix; shoaler (sic) portion of Scotch Bank; equivalent of Danish *Sandbordet*.

Sandbordet:
Sandboard Shoal, or Scotch Reef, at Bassin or Christiansted Harbor entrance, St. Croix.

Sandia:
Spanish name meaning "Watermelon," also spelled *Zandia*, applied to Waterlemon Cay, St. John. Described as *Cayuelo acantilado* (steep little cay).

Sandy Point Rock:
Elongated reef in West Gregerie Channel, with depths of 1 foot at northeast and 3 feet at 50 yards southwest, midway between Sandy Point and Gregerie Bank, 250 yards from each. Another reef, with 1-foot depth, lies between Sandy Point and Sandy Point Rock, called by Spanish *La Piedra de Punta Sandy*.

Santiago Chico:
Spanish name of Little St. James Island.

Santiago Grande:
Spanish name of Great St. James Island.

San Tomas Chico:
Group composed of Salt Cay and West Cay, St. Thomas. Spanish equivalent of "Little St. Thomas," but differently applied.

Savaan Eyland:
Dutch name of Savana Island.

Savana Island:
269 feet high, area 173.8 acres, with 0.6 acre for adjacent

Glossary of place names

rocks; on western side rise many tyre-palms (*Coco thrinax*). Over an area of 0.31 acres are several rocks awash and two bare, one 6 feet high, lat. 18° x 20' 35.4" (1,087 m), long. 65° x 04' 19.3" (567 m).

Savanah Island:
Variant spelling of name Savana Island.

Savanna:
Variant spelling of name Savana Island. Also, with alternative, "Green Island."

School-of-Fish:
Shoal, awash at low water, 100 yards from shore, southeast from Fortberg Hill, western side of Hurricane Hole, St. John.

Schorbomonoch Eyland:
Islet in the passage between St. Thomas (*Isaak de Klert punt*) and *St. Jan of Groot St. Jems* (St. James) Island. Same as Current Rock.

Schorbomanok:
Isle apparently same as Steven-May or Meeren Cay, but probably Current Rock, St. Thomas.

Scorpion Rock:
More usual, but less correct, name of Scorpion Rocks.

Scorpion Rocks:
Small shoal of coralheads, depth 3 fathoms, near center of St. Thomas Harbor entrance fairway, between Cowel Point and Juhlenfels Point. Also called Scorpion rock; Spanish, La Piedra Scorpion. Discovered in 1851 by H.M.S. Scorpion.

Scotch Bank:
Sandy shoal, in spots only 4 feet deep, extending from Fort Louise Augusta northeast 1 3/4 miles, forming eastern side of Christiansted Harbor approach and entrance. Also called Scotch Reef; Spanish, *Banco Escoces*; Danish, *Skotske Banke* (*Sandbordet*); Sandboard Shoal or Reef; and *Det grone wand* (the green water).

Scotch Reef:
Same as Scotch Bank, St. Croix; Scotch Shoal, more appropriate.

Senior Cay:
Varian of *Sinjo* or *Zinjo*, unless these last are corruption of the former. Same as Mingo Cay.

Shark Islet or Cay:
32 feet high, area 1.25 acres.

Sibbe Bay:
On northern shore of East End Peninsula St. John, 1/2 mile from East End Point. Called Sibbes Bay; identifies with Newfound Bay.

Singo:
Same as Mingo Cay.

Singo Key:
Same as Mingo Cay.

Sixfoot Ledge:
Rock-islet, area 0.22 acres, rising 6 feet above low-water, 270 yards east of Savana Island.

Skipper Jacobs Klippe:
Same as Skipper Jacob Rock.

Skipper Jacob Rock:
220 yards east of May Point, Steven Cay, Pillsbury Sound.

Sortklip:
See Blackrock.

Southwest Shoal:
Ledges, reefs, and shoals lying off south coast of Prince Quarter, St. Croix, 1 to 1/2 miles out, for distance of 3 miles, with 3 1/4 fathoms inshore, shoaling landward and eastward toward Krause point anchorage. Outside is another chain of dangerous reefs and breakers continuing east-northeast for 3 miles farther, known as Long Reef. West end of Southwest Shoal is called Southwest Reef.

Sprat Rock:
Double crag, area 0.15 acres, 240 yards west-northwest of Sprat Point, and marking east entrance of Sprat Bay, Water Island.

Steep Rock:
25 feet high, area 0.12 acres; only large detached rock on eastern shore of Little Hans Lollik. Descriptive designation, sides being steep and bold.

Stepmar Cay:
Same as Steven or Meeren Cay.

Steven Cay:
28 feet high; area 2.0 acres, not inclusive of May Rock. (Not *Meeren, Meeven, Mercy, Meren, Stepmar*, nor Steven May.)

Steven May:
Steven Cay.

Store James Eyland:
Great St. James Island. Trilingual compound: Danish, *Store* (Great); English, James; Dutch, *Eyland* (Island). Also, St. Jan.

Store St. James:
Danish name for Great St. James Island. Described as having a *bomuldsplantage* (cotton plantation).

Stragglers:
Rock islets southwest of St. James Island. Described as *penascos acantilados* (steep rocks).

Glossary of place names

Sula Cay:
50 feet high, area 1.9 acres. Frequented by brown boobies, *Sula leucogaster*.

Swei Bruder:
German equivalent of Two Brothers.

Target Rock:
Shore-rock just off Botany Point, St. Thomas. Once used as a rifle range.

Tatch Key:
Thatch Cay.

Ternera:
Spanish name of Calf Rock, 940 yards south of Deck Point, St. Thomas.

Teyer Kay:
Thatch Cay. Also: *Teyerkey, Teyerkeyen*.

Teyerkey:
Thatch Cay.

Teyerkeyen:
Thatch Cay.

Thatch Cay:
482 feet high, area 286.8 acres, exclusive of Lee Rock.

The Rock:
Bullhole Rock, west of Grass Cay.

Tiburon:
Spanish name of Shark Islet, off eastern end of St. Thomas.

Tip Rock:
Largest of the rocks called by the Spanish *Piedres sueltas*, southwest of Savana Island. Lat. 18° x 20' 11.6" (357 m), long. 65° x 05' 10.7" (315 m).

To Brødre:
Two Brothers Rocks, *De to Brødre*.

Tombstone Rock:
Conspicuous dark-gray boulder, 6 feet high, 2 feet wide; on sandy beach at Lerken Bay, St. Thomas. Danish, *gravsten* (tomb).

Touch Key:
Same as Thatch Cay.

Triangel:
Same as Triangle Rocks.

Triangle Rocks:
Group of three small rock clusters, midway between Green Cay and Muhlenfels Point, in St. Thomas Harbor approach. Outer Rock, 1 foot high, 635 yards offshore; Inner Rock, partially awash, 500 yards offshore; Barrel-of-Beef rock on east, 2 feet high, 415 yards offshore. Equivalents: Danish, *Trekant*; Dutch, *Drieboek (Dribut)*; German, *Tigon*; Spanish *El Triangulo* (sing.) or *Los Triangulos* (plural). Miscalled "The Triangles," whereas the three groups constituted only one triangle. "Triangle" (sing.) mistakenly described as *Blinde Klippen* (blind or sunken rocks).

Triangulo, El:
"The Triangle," Spanish name for Triangle Rocks.

Trunk Cay:
48 feet high, area 2.25 acres. Bluff shore; top covered with shrubbery.

Turkey Cay:
English equivalent for Kalkun Cay.

Turtleback Rock:
Area 0.012 acres, 12 feet high, 1/4 mile east-northeast of Footer Point at Water Bay entrance, 590 yards east-southeast of Coki Point, St. Thomas. (Not Turtle Back nor Turtle Rock.) Spanish, *Lomo Tortuga*.

Turtledove Cay:
50 feet high, area 3.78 acres. Covered with tall grass.

Turtle Dove Cay:
Less correct form of Turtledove Cay.

Turtledove Key:
Same as Turtledove Cay.

Two Brothers:
20 feet high, area 0.35 acres.

Tyer Kay:
Same as Teyer or Thatch Cay.

Usher Cay:
Point, projecting from mangrove shore 220 to 270 yards in northeast portion of Coral Harbor, St. John, and terminating in a 42-foot knoll, on which resides the government physician. Spelled also Usher's Cay or Usher's Quay.

Vaca, La:
Spanish name of Cow Rock, 1,000 yards south-southwest of Deck Point, St. Thomas.

Verde, Cay:
Spanish name of Green Cay, St. Croix.

Verde, Cayo:
Spanish equivalent of Green Cay or Thatch Cay, outside French Bay, southern shore of St. Thomas.

Verte, Isle:
French, "Green Isle" properly, Green Cay, but transferred to Buck Island, St. Croix, on early charts. Description then

Glossary of place names

appropriate, island forested with guayaco (*lignum vitae*) trees. See *Pocken-Eyland*.

VIRGIN POINT:
Southwestern extremity of Savana Island, toward Virgin Passage. See descriptions of Domkirk Rock and *Piedras Sueltas*.

VOGEL EYLAND:
Dutch, meaning "Bird Island," same as Little Flat Cay.

VOGEL KLIP:
Dutch name, meaning "Bird Rock." Designation of Kalkun Cay, also Little Flat Cay.

WATEREYLAND:
Dutch equivalent of Water Island.

WATER ISLAND:
491.4 acres, exclusive of Sprat Rock; highest hill 294 feet; indented by several small bays and covered with small trees and dense underbrush.

WATERLEMON CAY:
30 feet high, area 0.74 acres. Overgrown with brush and grass. Lat. 18° x 11' 08.6" (261 m), long. 64° x 43' 24" (709 m).

WATER LIMON KAY:
Waterlemon Cay, St. John.

WATER MELON CAY:
Split form of Watermelon Cay, properly.

WATERMELON CAY:
Usual nautical name of Waterlemon Cay, derived by a metathesis.

WAVE ROCK:
16 feet high, 16 yards wide; lat. 18° x 18' 40.3", long. 64° x 57' 12"; at base of 60-foot cliff and 203-foot hill, east shore of south end of Water Island.

WELK ROCKS:
Ledge, exposing group of 6 rocks, one 10 feet high, together having an area of nearly 1/2 acre, 1/4 mile east of St. James Cut, in Pillsbury Sound. From a gastropod, the welk or whelk, Latin *Bussinium*, Spanish, *Concha*; whence Spanish name of Rock, *La Roca de la Concha*. Spelled "Wilk Rock" by Scorpion.

WESSEL CAY:
Whistling Cay, variant of Wissel.

WEST CAY:
Area 40.3 acres; separated from Little St. Thomas only by a boat channel, Big Current Hole. Altitudes, 121 and 190 feet, respectively; the southern hill is 114 feet high.

WESTKEY:
Same as West Cay.

WHELK ROCK:
Same as Welk Rocks.

WHET-KABAI:
Creole equivalent of "White Horse."

WHISTLING CAY:
202 feet high, area 18.6 acres. Top, tree-clad; goat pasture.

WHITE HORSE:
Alternative name for Hans-Lollik Rock. Creole equivalent, *Whet-Kabai*; Spanish, *Caballo Blanco*; all alluding to the foaming breakers that resemble the streaming mane of a white race horse.

WHITE HORSE:
Same as Whitehorse Rock, St. Croix.

WHITEHORSE ROCK:
Dangerous reef, with everbreaking surf, 400 yards off Saltriver Point, St. Croix. Two-fathom boat channel inshore. Also called White Horse; Danish, *Hvidhest*; Spanish, *Caballo Blanco*; Creole, *Whet Kabai*; *Kuglen* (the cone).

WILK ROCK:
Same as Welk Rocks.

WISSEL KAY:
Whistling Cay, Dutch word meaning "change, exchange"; Danish, *Vexel*; *Wessel*, another spelling.

ZANDIA CAY:
Spanish, meaning "Watermelon"; variant of *Sandia*, applied to Waterlemon Cay, St. John.

ZINGO:
See Mingo.

ZWARTKLIP:
See Blackrock.

REFERENCES

Banks, R. C., McDiarmid, R. W. and Gardner, A. L. 1987. Checklist of vertebrates of the United State, the U. S. Territories, and Canada. U. S. Fish and Wildlife Resource Publication 166. 79 pp.

Bowden, M. J., Allen, J., Avey, D., Andrew, R., Rosen, M., Kanis, S., Lappen, E., and Skeels, R. 1968. Water Balance of a Dry Island. Geography Publications at Dartmouth No. 6. 89 pp.

Bowden, M. J., Fischman, N., Cook, P., Woody, J., Omasta, E. 1970. Climate, Water Balance, and Climatic Change in the North-West Virgin Islands. Caribbean Research Institute, University of the Virgin Islands. 127 pp.

Ewel, J. J., and Whitmore, J. L. 1973. The Ecological Life Zones of Puerto Rico and the U.S. Virgin Islands. Institute of Tropical Forestry, Rio Piedras, Puerto Rico. 72 pp. Forest Service research paper ITF-18.

Holdridge, L. R. 1947. Determination of world plant formations from simple climatic data. Science 105: 367-368.

Holdridge, L. R. 1967. Life Zone Ecology. Tropical Science Center. San Jose, Costa Rica. 206 pp.

MacArthur, R. H. and Wilson, E. O. 1967. The theory of island biogeography. Princeton Univ. Press. Princeton. 203 pp.

McGuire, W. J. 1925. Geographic Dictionary of the Virgin Islands of the United States. U.S. Coast and Geodetic Survey. 211 pp.

Odum, W.E., McIvor, C. C., and Smith, T. J., III. 1982. The ecology of the mangroves of south Florida: A community profile. U.S. Fish and Wildlife Service, Office of Biological Services, Washington, DC. 144 pp.

Philobosian, R. A. and Yntema, J. A. 1977. Annotated checklist of the Birds, Mammals, Reptiles and Amphibians of the Virgin Islands and Puerto Rico. Information Services at St. Croix. 48 pp.

Rivera, L. H., Frederick, W. D., Farris, C., Jensen, E. H., Davis, L., Palmer, C. D., Jackson, L. F., and McKinzie, W. E. 1970. Soil Survey of the Virgin Islands of the United States. U.S. Department of Agriculture. 78 pp.

Robertson, W. B. 1957. Biological report - Initial study and development survey, Virgin Islands National Park. National Park Service. 54 pp.

Index to Species

Bold, italicized numerals refer to photographs.

Acacia, *Acacia macracanthe,* ***26***, ***34***, 35, 49, 51, 59, 85, 109, 113, 117, 119, 131
African tulip tree, *Spathodea campanulata,* ***124***, 125
Agouti, *Dasyprocta aguti,* 14
Anole, 50, 133
   Barred anole, *Anolis stratulus,* 23, 41, 50, 53, 67, 69, 73, ***76***, 76, 77, 79, 81, 87, ***88***, 88, 89, 109, 113, 117, 119, 125, 131
   Crested anole, *Anolis cristatellus,* 23, 27, 29, 33, 35, 37, ***38***, 38, 39, 41, 45, 47, 49, 50, 53, 55, 57, 59, 61, 65, 67, 69, 71, 73, 77, 81, 83, 85, 87, 89, 97, ***98***, 98, 99, 101, 103, 107, 109, 111, 113, 115, 117, 119, 121, 125, 127, 129, 131
   Grass anole, *Anolis pulchellus,* ***22***, 22, 23, 25, 50, 61, 79, 81, 83, 117, 125
   St. Croix anole, *Anolis acutus,* 25, 63, ***94***, 94, 95
Antillean crested hummingbird, *Orthorynchus cristatus,* 103
Audubon's shearwater, *Puffinus iherminieri,* 37, ***102***, 102, 103
Bahama duck, *Anas bahamensis,* ***62***
Bananaquit, *Coereba flaveola,* 23, 103
Bay cedar, *Suriana maritima,* 29
Beach pea, *Canavalia maratima,* 57, 91, 99, 111, ***128***, 128, 129
Bellapple, *Passiflora laurifolia,* 127
Black-necked stilt, *Himantopus mexicanus,* ***60***, 88
Black rat, *Rattus rattus,* 21, 25, 27, 29, 33, 35, 39, 41, 45, 49, 61, 69, ***70***, 70, 71, 73, 87, 89, 117, 119
Blind snake, *Typhlops richardi,* ***108***, 108
Bridled tern, *Sterna anaethetus,* 21, 37, 41, ***42***, 42, 43, 47, 49, 53, 55, 57, 75, 105, 121
Bromeliad, *Bromelia,* ***46***, 47, ***82***, 83, 101, 133
Brown booby, *Sula leucogaster,* 16, 21, 36, 37, ***42***, 43, 49, 57, ***74***, 74, 75, 87, 105, ***114***, 114, 115
Brown pelican, *Pelecanus occidentalis,* 16, 25, ***40***, 41, 49, ***50***, 101, ***130***, 130, 131,
Buttonwood fruit, ***22***
Cactus, 23, 25, 29, 30, 67, 69, 73, 89, 95, 119, 131
   Dildo cactus, *Pilocereous royenii,* ***44***, 45, 63, 97, 99, 101
   Jumping cactus, *Opuntia repens,* 65, 91, 97, ***100***, 127
   Prickly pear cactus, *Opuntia sp.,* 49, 53, 54, 55, 63, 65, 75, ***76***, 77, 101, ***112***, 112, 127
   Tree cactus, *Opuntia rubescens,* 35, ***48***, 113
   Turkscap cactus, *Melocactus intortus,* 39, 45, ***46***, 47, 77, 85, 97, 99, 101, 103, ***104***, 104, 105, 111
   Woolly nipple cactus, *Mammillaria nivosa,* ***46***, 46, 47, 81, ***84***, 85, ***98***, 99
Cave bat, *Brachyphylla cavernarum,* ***86***, 86
Century plant, *Agave missionum,* ***58***, 59, ***68***, 69, 73, 117, 131
Clapper rail, *Rallus longirostri,* 23
Coconut palm, *Cocos nucifera,* 25, 39, 67, 69, 73, 79, ***94***, 95, 125
Cotton ginner gecko, *Sphaerodactylus beattyi,* ***24***, 25, 61, 63
Crab bush, *Clerodendrom aculeatum,* ***36***, 37, 49, 57, ***120***, 121, ***136***
Deer (*see* white-tailed deer)
Donkey, 67
Dwarf gecko, *Sphaerodactylus macrolepis,* 23, 27, 33, ***34***, 34, 35, 37, 39, 41, 47, 51, 53, 55, 57, 59, 61, 65, ***66***, 66, 67, 69, 71, 73, 79, 81, 85, 87, 89, 95, 101, 103, 107, 109, 113, 117, 121, 125, 127, 129, 131
Egret, 15, 16, 33, 101, 133
   Great egret, *Egretta alba,* 23, 132
   Reddish egret, *Egretta rufescens,* 132
   Snowy egret, *Egretta sula,* 23, ***62***, 63, ***94***, 113
Fig, *Ficus,* 16, 31, 37, 41, 49, ***56***, 57, 59, 75, 99
Fish poison, *Piscidia piscipula,* 127
Fishing bat, *Noctilio leporinus,* 87, ***116***, 116
Flamboyant, *Delonix regia,* 71
Frangipani, *Plumeria alba,* 25, 29, 35, 53, ***64***, 64, 65, 71, 97, 101, 109
Geiger, *Cordia spp.,* 125
Goat, 13, 18, 41, 49, 67, 87, 109, 117, 129
Grassquit, *Tiarus bicolor,* 23
Gray kingbird, *Tyrannus dominicensis,* 23, 35, 65, 71
Green iguana, *Iguana iguana,* 23, 33, ***68***, 69, 89, 125, 133
Green turtle, *Chelonia mydas,* ***24***, 24, 25
Ground dove, *Columbaigallina passerina,* 21, 23, 27, 35, 39, 47, 51, 55, 59, 65, 71, 81, 83, 97, 103, 115, 121, 129
Ground lizard, *Ameiva exsul,* 17, 23, 33, 49, 53, 55, 61, 67, 69, 73, 77, 79, 81, 83, ***84***, 84, 85, 87, 101, 107, 109, 117, 125
Guinea grass, *Panicum maximum,* 22, 35, 101, 103, 107
Gumbo limbo, *Bursera simaruba,* 29, ***40***, 41, 71, 97, 101, 119, 125, 127, 131
Haiti-haiti, *Thespesia populnea,* 51
Hawksbill turtle, *Eretmochelys imbricata,* 25, 47, 61, 67, 73, ***78***, 78, 79, 103
Hermit crab, *Coenobita clypeata,* ***92***, 92
Heron, 15, 16, 33, 101, 133, 137
   Great blue heron, *Ardea herodius,* 23, 63, ***122***, 123, 132
   Green-backed heron, *Butoroides striatus,* 23, 63, ***112***, 113
   Little blue heron, *Egretta caerula,* ***22***, 23, ***62***, 63, ***112***, 113
   Tricolor heron, *Hydranassa tricolor,* 63, 113
   Yellow-crowned night heron, *Nycticorax violaceus,* 63, ***98***, 99, ***136***
House gecko, *Hemidactylus mabouia,* 23, 34, ***58***, 58, 51, 59, 69, 71, 73, 77, 81, 83, 89, 103
Hummingbird, *Eulampis holosericeus,* 15, 23, 71, 133
Humpback whale, *Megaptera novaeangliae,* ***40***, 40, 41
Iguana (*see* green iguana)
Inkberry, *Randia aculeata,* 33, 71, 93, 97
Jamaican caper, *Caparis cyanocephala,* 85, 127
Jamaican fruit-eating bat, *Artibeus jamaicansis,* 86, 87, ***118***, 118, 119
Kestrel, *Falco sparvarius,* ***60***

Killdeer, *Charadrius vociferus*, 135
Kingbird (*see* gray kingbird)
Laughing gull, *Larus atricilla*, 20, 21, 37, **44**, 44, 45, 47, 53, 55, 57, **78**, 79, 87, 91, 99, 103, 113, 121, 123
Leatherback turtle, *Dermochelys coriacea*, 25, **72**, 72, 73
Leatherleaf, *Stigmaphyllon periplacifolium*, 39, **52**, 57, **74**, 75, 91, 93
Lichens, **70**
Lignum vitae, *Dermochelys coriacea*, **24**, 25
Limber caper, *Capparis flexuosa*, 97, 99, 101
Magnificent frigatebird, *Fregata magnificens*, **24**, 25, **48**, 48, 49, **104**, 105
Maho, *Hibiscus tiliaceus*, 67, 113
Mahogany, *Swietenia mahogoni*, 71, **94**, 95
Mampo, *Torrubia fragrans*, 29, 33, 67, **86**, 125, 127
Manchineel, *Hippomane mancinella*, 25, 61, 63, 67, 71, **80**, 81, **96**, **100**, 100, 101, 103
Mangrove, 16, 17, 23, 95, 101
   Black mangrove, *Avicennia germinans*, 15, 17, 47, 77, 101, 103
   Buttonwood, *Conocarpus erectus*, 15, 17, 38, 39, 45, 51, 63, 65, 91, 123
   Red mangrove, *Rhizophora mangle*, 15, 17, **22**, 23, **32**, 33, **88**, 89, 101, **132**
   White mangrove, *Laguncularia racemosa*, 15, 17, **100**, 101
Maran, *Croton sp.*, 35, 59, 65, 85, 101, 109, 117, 127
Marblewood, *Cassine xylocarpa*, 71
Masked booby, *Sula dactylatra*, **36**, 36, 37, 43, 49, **114**, 115
Mongoose (*see* small Indian mongoose)
Mountain dove (*see* Zenaida dove)
Mouse, *Mus musculus*, 33, 41, 61, 69, 73, 87, 119
Nicker bean, *Caesalpinia divergens*, **102**, 127
Noddy tern, *Anous stolidus*, **30**, 30, 31, 37, 41, 43, 49, 55, 57, 75, 103, 105, 121
Orchid
   Christmas orchid, *Epidendrum ciliare*, **108**
   Cliff orchid, *Encyclia bifidum*, 24
   Grass orchid, *Tetramicra elegans*, **32**, 33
   White dancing lady orchid, *Oncidium variagatum*, **66**
   Yellow dancing lady orchid, *Oncidium prionochylum*, **66**
Oystercatcher, *Haematopus palliatus*, **20**, 21, 45, 55, 63, 65, 75, 91, 99, 137
Pelican (*see* brown pelican)
Peregrine falcon, *Falco peregrinus*, **56**, 57, **60**
Physic nut, *Jatropha gossypifolia*, 71
Pigeon (*see* white-crowned pigeon)
Pinguin, *Bromelia pinguin*, **82**, 83
Pink cedar, *Tabebuia heterophylla*, 65
Portulaca, *Portulaca*, 91, **96**, 97, 99
Puerto Rican garden snake, *Arrhyton exiguis*, 69
Puerto Rican racer, *Alsophis puertoricensis*, **26**, 27, 29, 33, 37, 41, 47, 59, 61, 67, 69, 73, 79, 81, 83, 85, 87, 89, 103, 109, 117, 121, 125, 129
Queen conch, *Strombus gigas*, 81
Rabbit, 79
Rat (*see* black rat)
Red-billed tropicbird, *Phaethon aethereus*, 27, **28**, 28, 30, 31, 33, 37, 41, 43, 49, 55, 59, 67, 75, 81, 85, 87, 105, 115, 123, 125, 129
   nest of, **84**
Red-footed booby, *Sula sula*, **48**, 49, **56**, 56, 57, 115
Red-footed tortoise, *Geochelone carbonaria*, **124**, 124, 125
Red-tailed hawk, *Buteo jamaicensis*, **126**
Roof bat, *Molossus molossus*, **106**, 106, 107
Roseate tern, *Sterna dougallii*, 21, 33, 39, 43, 47, **52**, 52, 53, 55, 75, 81, 91, **92**, 103, 105, **110**, 111, 117, 121, 123
Royal tern, *Sterna maxima*, **54**, 54, 55, **122**, 123
St. Croix gecko, 34
St. Croix ground lizard, *Ameiva polops*, **62**, 62, 63, 95
St. Thomas tree boa, *Epicrates monensis*, 41, **60**, 60
St. Thomas worm lizard, *Amphisbaena fenestrata*, 61, **108**, 108, 109
Sally lightfoot crab, *Grapsus grapsus*, **122**, 122
Samphire flower, *Philoxerus vermicularis*, **50**
Sandwich tern, *Sterna sandvicensis*, 55, **90**, 91
Scaly-naped pigeon, *Columba squamosa*, **109**
Sea grape, *Cocoloba uvifera*, **20**, 21, 33, 35, 37, **38**, 38, 39, 41, 45, 51, 59, 65, 67, 77, 93, 97, 109, 111, 115, 121, 123, 127, 129
Sea hibiscus, *Hibiscus tiliaceus*, 71
Sea lavender, *Tournefortia graphalodes*, 29
Sea purslane, *Sesuvium portulacastrum*, 29, 31, 39, **42**, 43, **90**, 90, 91, 99, 121, 127
Slipperyback skink, *Mabuya sloani*, 27, 29, 33, 63, 77, 103, **106**, 107, 125
Small Indian mongoose, *Herpestes auropuntatus*, 25, **82**, 82, 83
Smooth-billed ani, *Crotophaga ani*, 53, 83
Soldier crab, *Coenobita clypeatus*, **100**
Songbirds, 63
Sooty tern, *Sterna fuscata*, 47, 55, 57, **102**, 102, 103, **120**, 120, 121
Tamarind fruit, **68**
Tamarind tree, *Tamarindus indica*, 35, 95
Tan-tan, *Leucaena leucocephala*, 22, 95, 103
Top shell (*see* whelk)
Tree boa (*see* St. Thomas tree boa)
Turpentine tree, *Bursera simaruba*, 25
Turtle grass, *Thalasia testudinum*, 23
Turtle, endangered, 11
Tyre palm, *Coccothrinax alta*, 59, 67, 73, 109, **116**, 117, **118**, 119, 131
Vireo, *Vireo sp.*, 23
Warbler, *Dendroica petechia*, 133
Whelk, *Cittarium pica*, 20, **100**
White-cheeked pintail duck, *Anas bahamensis*, 17, 29, 33, 47, 55, 61, 63, 103, 111, 133, **134**,
White-tailed deer, *Odocoileus virginianus*, 23, 33, 45, 47, 61, **80**, 80, 89, 101, 129
White-tailed tropicbird, *Phaethon lepturus*, **32**, 32, 33, 37, 41, 47, 49, 73, 81, 87, 125, 129
Wilson's plover, *Charadrius wilsonia*, 23
Zenaida dove, Zenaida aurita, 21, 23, 27, 31, 35, 37, 41, 43, 47, 51, 55, 57, 59, 71, 75, 77, 97 103, 107, 111, 115, 121, **128**

General Index

Bold, italicized numerals refer to photographs.

Agriculture, 13, 73
Big Current Hole, 129
Booby Rock, 16, *20-21*, 21
Botany Point, 49
Bovoni Cay, *22-23*, 23, 33, 89
Breeding seasons, 10
Buck Island (near St. Croix), *24-25*, 25
Buck Island (near St. Thomas), *26-27*, 27, 29
Burning, 14, 27, 37, 73
Cabes Point, 111
Calf Rock, *136*
Capella Island, 26, 27, *28-29*, 29, 57
Cartanza, 27
Carvel Rock, 16, *30-31*, 31
Cas Cay, *32-33*, 33, 89
Christiansted, 25, 95
Christmas Cove, 61
Cinnamon Bay, 35
Cinnamon Cay, *34-35*, 35
Climate, 11-12, 18
Cockroach Cay, *36-37*, 37, 43, 115
Cocoloba Cay, *38-39*, 39
Colonization, 14-15
Compass Point, 101
Competition, 9
Congo Cay, *40-41*, 41
Coral gardens, 27
Cotton plantation, 61
Cow Rock, *136*
Cricket Rock, 37, *42-43*, 43
Current Rock, *44-45*, 45
Daisy, 47
Denis Bay, 93
Desertification, 18
Distribution of species, 14
Dog Island, 16, *46-47*, 47, 57
Domestic animals, 73, 87
Durloe Cays, 96, 99
Dutch settlement, 65, 67
Dutchcap Cay, 37, *48-49*, 49
East Bay, 117
European colonization, 13
Eva Bay, 117
Evapo-transpiration, 11, 13
Evolution, 14
Extinction, 9, 13, 24
Fish Bay, 39
Fish Cay, *50-51*, 51, 61
Flamingo Bay, 125
Flanagan Island, *52-53*, 53
Flat Cay, *54-55*, 55
Fort Louis Augusta, 63
Fort Sofia Frederika, 95

French Bay, 65
Frenchcap Cay, *56-57*, 57
Grass Cay, *58-59*, 59, 85
Grazing, 13, 33
Great St. James Island, 45, *60-61*, 61
Green Cay (St. Croix), 14, *62-63*, 63, 95
Green Cay (St. Thomas), *64-65*, 65
Greenhouse effect, 15
Hans Lollick Island, 13, *66-67*, 67
Hassel Island, *68-69*, 69
Henley Cay, *70-71*, 71, 97, 99
HMS Rhone, 27
Hognest Bay, 93
Hognest Point, 83
Indians, 13, 25
    artifacts of, 41, 63
Inner Brass Island, *72-73*, 73
Insolation, 11, 13
Island effect, 13
Islands, oceanic, 14
Jasper, *70*
Jersey Bay, 23, 101
Kalkun Cay, *74-75*, 75
Krause Cay and Lagoon, *17*, 17, 135
Lang Bank, 14
Leduck Island, 16, *76-77*, 77
Leinster Point, 127
Lilac, 105
Little Flat Cay, *54*, 55
Little Hans Lollick Island, *78-79*, 79, 91
Little St. James Island, 47, *80-81*, 81
Lovango Cay, 41, *82-83*, 83, 85
Mammals, fossil record of, 14
Manglars, 17, 101, *132-133*, 133
Manmade/destroyed islands, *134-135*, 135
Mingo Cay, 59, *84-85*, 85
Monito Island, 37
Moor Point, 77
Outer Brass Island, 40, *86-87*, 87
Patricia Cay, 23, 33, *88-89*, 89
Pelican Cay, *90-91*, 91
Perkins Cay, *92-93*, 93
Petroglyphs, 41
Pillsbury Sound, 113
Pollution, 9
Population, human, 9
Pre-Columbian period, 12
Privateer Point, 53
Protestant Cay, 14, 62, *94-95*, 95
Pull Point, 63
Rainfall, 11, 13, 15, 18
Ram Head, 21, 77
Ramgoat Cay, *96-97*, 97
Rata Cay, *98-99*, 99

Red Point, 33, 55
Refugia, 14
Resources, management of, 9
Rotto Cay, *100-101*, 101
Rough Out Point, 87
Run-off, 11, 13
Rupert Rock, *9*
Ruth Cay, *135*,
Saba Island, 55, *102-103*, 103, 121
Sabbat Point, 77
Sail Rock, 16, *104-105*, 105
St. Croix, 11, 13, 14, 17, 50, 62, 80, 95, 135
St. John, 11, 12, 13, 21, 35, 39, 43, 50, 53, 77, 83, 93, 113, 119
St. Thomas, 11, 13, 16, 23, 36, 37, 43, 45, 50, 57, 61, 67, 75, 80, 89, 101, 105, 107, 111, 115, 117, 129
Salt Cay, 49, *106-107*, 107, 129
Salt pond, 15, 25, 47, 69, 107, 125
Sandy Point, 25
Savana Island, 12, 105, *108-109*, 109
Savanna Passage, 75
Scuba diving, 21, 27, 29, 31, 37, 57, 67, 81, 113, 117, 125
Sea level, 15
Shark Island, *110-111*, 111
Shipwrecks, 61, 85, 125
Shoreline, 11
Signal lights, 25, 27, 45
Snorkeling, 21, 25, 27, 29, 35, 51, 53, 57, 67, 77, 79, 83, 97, 113, 119, 125
Soil temperature, 13
Soil types, 10, 16
Species and moisture requirements, 13
Species, introduced, 9
Spoil island, 18
Steven Cay, *112-113*, 113
Submarines, 27
Sula Cay, 37, *114-115*, 115
Temperature, soil, 13
Tertiary period, 14
Thatch Cay, 59, *116-117*, 117
Tradewinds, 11
Trunk Cay, *118-119*, 119
Turtle Rock, *137*,
Turtledove Cay, 103, *120-121*, 121
Two Brothers, *122-123*, 123
U.S. Buck Island National Wildlife Refuge, 27
U.S. Virgin Islands
  area of, 11
  climate of, 11
  historic changes of, 12-15
Unvegetated rocks, *136-137*, 137
Vegetation, classifications of, 11-12
Water Island, *124-125*, 125
Water table, 13
Waterlemon Cay, *126-127*, 127
West Cay, 107, *128-129*, 129
Whistling Cay, *130-131*, 131
Wind, effect of on vegetation, 12
Wye, 27
Xerophytes, 12